The Limitless Spirit
of the Martial Arts

The Limitless Spirit

Spirit

of the Martial Arts

Marilyn Fierro, Hanshi

Apsos Publishing | Pennsylvania, USA

Apsos Publishing
Apsos LLC
Pennsylvania, USA

ISBN-13: 978-0692851661 (Apsos Publishing)
ISBN-10: 0692851666

WARNING: Martial arts training is a serious and potentially dangerous endeavor. All training should be done under the careful guidance of a competent instructor.

The information contained in this book is for research purposes only. The reader assumes all risk of training and absolves the author and publisher of liability.

Cover Photo Design Credit: Inspired by the original article featured in The Taekwondo Times.

The cover photo focuses around the classic Yin Yang of Chinese origin. It is central to the cover just as spiritual study has been central to Fierro Sensei's development as a person and martial artist. The Yin Yang breaks into dozens of birds, representing the limitless ways in which energy can influence our daily lives. The central bird represents Fierro Sensei herself during her journey. The cover also features the famed Mizugami of Isshin Ryu in the background, watching carefully over Fierro Sensei and all karateka.

CONTENTS

Dedication

This book is dedicated to:

Soke Shimabuku Tatsuo -

For creating the style I love so much

Isshinryu Karate (One Heart Way).

My Sensei Hanshi Nick Adler -

For making this impossible dream possible.

My Okinawa Sensei Hanshi Uezu Angi -

For your kindness and care.

My Family –

For putting up with my travels and

never-ending desire to learn and grow.

And to all

who find themselves on a similar path -

May you find encouragement in

one small spark of recognition.

Acknowledgements

If my life had been any different I could never have become who I am today. I met my husband when I was 16 and impressionable. If he had been anything other than the person he is, my story would be quite different. Whatever I chose to do was not met with discouragement, but with support.

I first wish to thank my husband, Ralph, and sons Michael and Steven, for their understanding as I explored my own possibilities.

I thank my first karate teacher, Dan, for encouraging me to do better rather than tell me how terrible I looked. Although I did not stay in his system it was a springboard into my more formal training. I discovered Isshinryu Karate through another instructor -Jimmy, who after recognizing I intended to train, was also patient and encouraging.

My martial arts journey began the day I walked into Adler Sensei's dojo, was demoted to white belt, and continues still today. To the man who has been my Sensei since 1974, taught me what martial arts was about and introduced me to so many great and wonderful instructors along the way, my heartfelt and deep gratitude.

There are so many people who deserve my thanks and as I put my words to paper I hope to highlight some of those who stand out in my memory. Through martial arts you meet people of all backgrounds, color, ethnicity and gender; but we are all Karate-Ka. Karate people sharing the same love and goals.

This book is a journey of thanks and blessings. Thank you, my dear reader, for following along with one person's thoughts and experiences.

Foreword

Mike Stone

Reading Marilyn Fierro's new book brought back many mixed emotions of my own personal journey through life and the martial arts. Her accounts through her childhood and life offer an incredible story of persistence, courage, determination, passion, and a strong desire to be our best in any given situation. It is especially gratifying and satisfying to read the names of wonderful people I have met through my personal friendship with Marilyn over these many years.

I love how she was willing to learn, then teach, and now continue to share her knowledge and wisdom acquired from her hardships, struggles, disappointments, and her willingness never to accept being less than she can be. I especially love the chapters on the positive universal laws and how she has applied them in her life to create a life of her own personal preferences and confidently made those choices to create the wonderful outcomes she has experienced.

I most highly recommend anyone and everyone to feel a sense of greater potential not yet achieved and to be inspired by her life's lessons. everyone can benefit from reading this inspirational and motivational contribution to the martial arts and the world in general. It is also a great book for women to aspire to what is possible even when society created limitations and boundaries for women.

Thank you Marilyn for your contribution to all of us.

Much Aloha,

Mike Stone

Retired Karate Competitive Champion, Fight Choreographer, Motivational Speaker

Foreword

Ann-Marie Heilman

As part of the same martial arts scene about which Ms. Fierro has so eloquently written, I can attest that Marilyn Fierro IS and WAS one the finest practitioners and teachers I have known. As females, we both entered the arts when women were not easily accepted into dojos but were offered only self-defense courses. However, both of us, not even knowing each other at the time, managed to work our way into a regular karate program.

Our friendship goes back many years and I can't remember our initial meeting but I know when we "touched hearts". It was on the playing field of a tournament and I was in the black belt weapons division waiting to compete. I used the tonfa for competition (because I had been told "you can't win with the tonfa" and I wanted to put that lie to rest!) Here comes another black belt woman – with a pair of tonfa! Rather than being competitors we became each other's cheerleader. Much to the annoyance of some male competitors, we were whispering and giving each other advice instead of staring down the competition with surly looks. From that time onward Marilyn and I became great friends and even better spiritual allies.

She is always in my heart as I am in hers and I can't imagine life in martial arts without her. We have traveled the same Path – just on slightly different and complementary tracks to the point of both studying kobudo (weapons) under Odo Seikichi Sensei . It is a small and blessed world that we live in.

As you read through this wonderful book please know that every word of it comes from Marilyn's heart to your heart. She has managed to funnel all of the knowledge that she has gained through careful study with the best there was and is. She blends it with discoveries of her own training in martial arts and spiritual work to share with her students and all ready to receive it. This then is the story of how she did it....

Ann-Marie Heilman

9th Dan Okinawa Kenpo Karate and Kobudo

Foreword

Fumio Demura

I met Marilyn Fierro many years ago. She is one of those people who is an example of how martial arts can enrich any person's life. She has achieved so much through her training, both in gaining expertise and also, and more importantly, in applying the many lessons she has learned to all parts of her life. Marilyn has done so much to build purpose and joy in her life through martial arts, and that is the true goal of training.

Martial arts is an essential part of my whole life. Of course, there is value in the knowledge of the physical elements, and I have been most fortunate to have been able to train in and teach a range and depth of expertise that I hope has benefited all of my students, both within my own organization and also through countless seminars. However, there are unlimited ways in which martial arts training offers benefits that are entirely separate from the physical. Training helps students develop character, learn to overcome difficulties, realize their potential...the list is endless.

Now Marilyn has added this new layer to her joy in martial arts, by sharing her experiences through her book. She is an example to others who might not have thought themselves able to explore the world of martial arts. She is an example to others of how the many lessons learned while training can impact every part of a person's life, and can help any student become successful. Success to me means that a person has developed their character to find happiness and joy by becoming a truly good person, as an individual and as a part of their family and their community. I hope you enjoy Marilyn's book, and find much to think about...much that can add happiness to your own life.

Shihan Fumio Demura

9th Dan Shito-Ryu Karate-Do GenbuKai, Stunt Choreographer, Author

Foreword

Willie Adams and Nick Adler

In 2008 At the KIAI Grand Nationals I (Marilyn Fierro) was awarded the Legion Of Honor by Master Willie Adams. What a surprise and honor to have received it. You can see a video of the presentation on Youtube by looking for "Kyoshi Fierro Legion of Honor 2008". With your indulgence I would like to share the words of Master Adams and my Sensei Master Adler with you as it is one of the rare occasions something so special was recorded for me.

MASTER ADAMS: "Legion of Honor, this is the second highest award Legion of Honor. This person I have known for many -many -many years and I have seen this individual compete all over the United States. Never says no - anything you ask this person to do she will - can you help judge - Yes I will help judge - this individual has competed throughout the country and this individual, she is one of the highest ranking women in the martial arts in the United States and well respected throughout the whole country. Everybody knows her, West Coast - East Coast everybody knows her.

The Legion of Honor goes to Kyoshi Marilyn Fierro - ::: Applause::: She sets the standard for women in the martial arts throughout the country in the martial arts. She always carries herself with pride and dignity and she can run a ring, I don't care if it is heavyweight men's black belt division - she demands respect - she doesn't have to push her way around they respect her."

MASTER NICK ADLER: "Ms. Fierro has been with me for almost 35 years, she's had her own school for over 20 some odd years, she's been promoted by me, Master Nagle, and Master Uezu. She has a teaching certificate from Okinawa. She's in the Jewish Sports Hall of Fame, she wrote articles ...you name it she's done it. She's my right-hand person, she helps me run all my tournaments, camps, and seminars. If I have to have something done right I know who to go to and I've always been very -very proud of her she came up in a very -very tough dojo - it didn't matter if you were a guy or a girl. When she competed she competed against men because they didn't have woman's divisions especially in weapons. She did very - very well and I am very -very proud of her." ::applause::

Foreword

Karate Instructor Still Defying Skeptics

Makes History With Induction Into Sports Hall of Fame

by Tom Allegra

Smithtown News Sports April 3, 1997 Pg. 24

Re-written with permission from the Smithtown News

Most people are blind enough to believe karate is simply a "man's sport." They haven't met Marilyn Fierro.

Fierro - student, instructor, and historian martial arts and owner/chief instructor of the Smithtown Karate Academy - continues to prove her skeptics wrong. She recently received her seventh degree black belt in Okinawan Isshinryu Karate to become the highest ranked woman in the sport. In addition Fierro will become only the second woman to enter the New York Jewish Sports Hall of Fame at the Fifth Annual Induction Ceremonies April 6th. And although the 54 - year - old Fierro says her curiosity of self-defense spawned her interest in karate, she admits it was others' doubts that pushed her not only to become involved with the sport but to succeed with flying colors.

"Every one of my friends said 'Ha Ha! You can't do this. Women don't do this." Fierro recalls of her peers initial response to her taking up of karate 25 years ago.

"Never tell a woman what she can't do."

Not only has Fierro moved up in the ranks from her original goal of earning a brown belt, but she has become an integral member of the Long Island Community. In 1994 she was runner up in the Long Island Film and Video Awards for her 56 minute video entitled "Woman's Attack Prevention program with Marilyn Fierro." After she presented this program to the N.Y. State Board of Education in November 1996, 11 high schools have added it to their physical education repertoire. Commack was the first to adopt this logical self-defense course, and was followed by the likes of Smithtown, Kings Park, Northport, and Huntington high schools.

Educating others in self-defense, however, is only one of the many lessons in life Fierro has taught her students over the years.

"She's a person of honor, of respect, esteem, honesty and trustworthiness." said 34- year old James Flynn, a Smithtown resident who studied under Sensei Fierro and whose four-year old son is now involved in her Little Dragons program. "Just being around her, you learn all those things."

Flynn continued: "She was a great instructor. She taught me a lot about not only the skills but about the philosophy, maturity, growing up and respect. She taught pacifism as opposed to aggression...she loves to teach and she's very good at what she does... She leaves a mark on your life."

Fierro currently instructs approximately 60 students at her academy on Main Street. One of those, is John Bolton, a Smithtown resident and 1996 graduate of SUNY Stony Brook. Bolton 22, has worked with Fierro for 11 years and became a Third Degree Black Belt - the minimum rank one must hold in order to instruct - in December of 1995. Although Bolton himself instructs at the "dojo" - the Japanese term for school - he knows there is always something to learn from Fierro.

"She's helped a lot of people fulfill their full potential," said Bolton who claims Fierro can teach her students "how to overcome limitations." I know she's made an impact on a lot of people's lives, especially my own."

Making that kind of positive impact is one reason teaching Isshinryu Karate is worthwhile for Fierro. Her selection for the New York Jewish Sports Hall of Fame is an indication that she's moving in the right direction.

"It tells me that I'm doing something to touch peoples' lives and to motivate them so they can be the best they can be," said Fierro of the honor stating she didn't even know she was nominated. She helped earn herself the recognition as director of the karate program at the Suffolk Youth Community Center in Commack (where the induction will be held) since 1984 and as organizer of the 1995 karate tournament at the Maccabi Youth Games. "The more opportunities I have to make a difference in peoples' lives, then I'm succeeding at what I'm doing on this earth."

That doesn't mean that Fierro believes there is a pinnacle to reach. In fact, one saying on a wall in her dojo reads: "Once you think you're on the road to mastery, you've already lost your path."

Her promotion to a higher level Black Belt was a perfect opportunity for her to be content with the status quo. But she wasn't.

"Does that mean you've achieved all your goals?," Fierro asked herself about her recent advance to Seventh Degree, which she dubbed her "major accomplishment." Her reply: "It doesn't. Just keep doing the things you love and keep trying to do better."

And anybody knows one enjoys doing what they do best. "Doing something you love and being able to share that with others," Fierro said "is a way to grow as a person." Fierro herself admits she would not have blossomed into the martial artist she is today without the help of her few supporters. Among those is her husband Ralph.

"If my husband had joined the rest of the people that said I shouldn't do it, I wouldn't have done it," she said. And of Hanshi Nick Adler, her Isshinryu instructor and the original owner of the Smithtown Academy, she said: "If he wouldn't have taught me how to be strong and less sensitive I might not have done it. He gave me the independence to grow as a martial artist, to grow as a person."

Fierro - who grew up in the Bronx before finishing

the construction of her Kings Park house in 1968 - began to come into her own in karate in the early 1980's. In November 1982 she took first place in the weapons division (between both men and women) and was promoted to Third Degree Black Belt on that same day. Before she assisted Adler in opening the Smithtown Karate Academy in 1978, Fierro worked as a licensed medical technician in a New York City hospital.

But it wasn't until the most recent decade that Fierro's hard work paid off with higher levels of recognition. In June 1995 she received an Outstanding Contribution Award from the American Okinawan Karate Association. In March 1996 she received a Legion of Honor by Adler's Centurion Association and in September 1996 she became the World Head of Family Sokeship Council Master Instructor in the Council's Hall of Fame. She admits she has done all of this without the god-given talents and coordination that many participants do have.

Ironically, being a woman in what many still call a "man's sport" has actually benefited Fierro in many ways.

Prologue

One day a wealthy man who loved cats went to a famous Japanese painter and asked him to create a painting of a cat. He returned several months later for his painting but was told to come back in three months. After three more months, he returned only to be told once again to come back.

Finally, a year had passed and the man returned for his painting. Still nothing was finished, but this time the artist took up his brush and quickly created the most beautiful painting of a cat the man had ever seen.

"Why have I waited a year for this when it took you only a few seconds to create it?" Asked the man.

With that, the artist opened a cabinet and out fell many paintings - all were of cats. You see, in some way or another we are constantly working on our masterpiece, but some of us never get around to creating it.

"A journey of a thousand miles starts with a single step," says Lao Tsu in the Tao Te Ching. Yet often that single step is the hardest one to take. As Mike Stone says, "The only time to do it is NOW!" And, thanks to him and Taina - today is now. I have a closet full of those discarded paintings or notes on what I would like to see in a book. The ideas aren't really new, just my way of seeing things and certainly something I wish to share with anyone traveling along a similar path.

Change and growth are evident all around us. Buildings are going up; land contours moving, seasons changing and life itself a never changing cycle. Not quite as obvious, but equally as important, is the change going on constantly within ourselves. Every living thing is growing ...new cells are changing and developing. If we are not growing then we are not living. If we are not open to ideas, if we do not share and teach, we greatly inhibit this growth.

 It is through the sharing of knowledge that we can create growth and energy. If simply wrapped in a box for special occasions, knowledge is not only lost, but greatly deprived of its chance to increase.

According to the Hagakure Bushido, "There is no end to training. Once you begin to feel that you are masters, you are no longer on the way you are to follow." This is not to say there are no masters, but rather, the way to mastery is an endless cycle of learning, teaching, sharing and growing.

 As a Kyu rank, we strive very hard to attain the "ultimate" rank of Black Belt. Kyu ranks start at ten and work their way through diligence to one. Dan ranks begin at one and work their way up accordingly. SHODAN...it is not the ultimate...nor the end. It is a beginning by which we first discover our responsibility to the Martial Arts, to Ourselves and to Others. We begin as a white belt, and our obi darkens with experience until Black Belt. We then begin again with a dark obi, and as the years wear on so does our obi, until once again it is white. A full circle has been completed.

Through the years, hopefully we have shared our acquired knowledge, and by this sharing, we find that an energy is created...an energy of growth. Thus, through the sharing of energies, student and teacher become one and with each other, and a bond is formed; a bond of loyalty, love and mutual respect.

For me, training in martial arts was a turning point on a meandering path that certainly lacked in direction. I was on a quest to live up to...something. I always seemed to have an empty space in me.

You see, I was so busy living up to everyone's image of what I should be all my life that I never had a chance to find myself. Karate, it turned out, was the path to *me*. Through this vehicle, I learned what I was about and gained deeper insight to the workings of others. I grew to become a teacher, and through teaching, learned more than I could have on my own. I had begun to grow as a spiritual individual and once I discovered karate I was also able to see the inherent spirituality within its teaching.

This book is the culmination of all those pieces of paper falling out of my closet, and drawers, and boxes and corners. I hope you find something within worth taking with you on your journey.

"Life isn't a destination - it's a journey.

We all come upon unexpected curves and turning points,

mountain tops and valleys.

Everything that happens to us shapes who we are becoming,

and in the adventure of each day,

we discover the best in ourselves."

- Hallmark Card

"If you are to see into a man's spirit, the best place to watch is his eyes, as they will give away his actions."

-Master Shimabuku Tatsuo

Part 1 – My Story

Marilyn Fierro

Chapter 1 – Finding Karate

Our experiences form the core of who we are and how we respond to life's challenges. What if we are born with a certain destiny, guiding us toward the experiences we didn't know we needed?

Some call it Karma. Some call it Fate. Others just believe in coincidence.

What I know is that one day I joined a health club to lose weight and discovered martial arts through a self-defense program. It changed my life forever.

But that's where I ended up. How I got there is a question that bares some explanation, as it may reveal why the discovery of karate was so fortuitous, and so life changing for me.

Like most people I do not remember much until about eighth grade, other than little snippets of life events. The rest are feelings. I remember feelings more vividly than names, faces, or places. When viewing a movie, I take in the scene and how it makes me feel. My life is no different.

I was born in 1942, a year after Pearl Harbor. WWII was in full swing and many things were hard to come by. I do not remember any of this. My father had been in the Navy. When he returned home he got sick (Rheumatic Heart Disease). Such a simple thing that is totally curable today.

I was two years old when he passed. My mother had no income and eventually lost our apartment, basically putting us out on the street. My Russian-born grandfather would not help her. In his mind, my mother was no longer his responsibility.

Eventually, we moved to a small apartment. We were so poor that Mom took the curtains off the living room wall and made Mother/Daughter outfits for us. People saw them and loved them, so she began sewing clothing and doing alterations at home where she could be with

Marilyn in 1944, the year her father passed away.

the children. She was an artist and a baker, so she made beautiful wedding cakes and decorated cakes for special occasions. I remember very little of that time other than sitting by her playing with my toys as she sewed away. But I do remember how it made me feel.

Mother and daughter spending time together.

Mom re-married when I was seven. My brother and I were not there for this. Children were to be seen and not heard in those days and certainly in my family we were given very little information. The ceremony occurred while we were at school; when I came home I didn't find her there waiting for me.

In school we had to do air raid drills, to learn how to hide under the desks in case of an enemy attack. My brother, being five years older, was in a different school by then and I feared that we would be separated and alone.

Many weeks of my summers were spent with my grandparents in Cornwall on the Hudson in New

York, off the Old Storm King Highway. I loved animals and felt blessed to live across the street from a small farm. I used to go there every day and help care for the animals, but my real love was always the horses. I would muck out stalls just to be near them and have an occasional opportunity to ride.

The Cornwall home where the family often spent their summers.

One day when I went down to breakfast, my grandfather said, "Get those horses off my lawn." I looked out, and sure enough, the neighbor's entire herd had escaped and were on our front lawn. To this day, I do not know how at 9 1/2 or so, I figured out how to catch the leader of the pack in order to bring them back.

There was a mare that was the lead's mate and she was a very gentle horse. I decided to go up to her and take her halter. She was very sweet and had no problem with my presence, so I carefully walked up to the stallion, with her right behind me, and he let me take his halter as well. I started walking with the two horses and the rest of the herd followed. This was a Sunday morning and people were getting ready for church. At that time there was no thruway, just the narrow two lane Storm King highway which ran in front of my grandparents' house. The horses spread out across the road and I had traffic backed up quite a ways. Luckily, the farm was not far and the farmer, who was also the Major of Cornwall and veterinarian for West Point, was leaving for church and saw me coming. He brought the horses in and that afternoon took me with his daughter out for the day to celebrate. It was the best thing I had ever done up to that point.

My attachment to my mother was always extremely strong. She was all I had for the first part of my life. When she got sick and needed gallbladder surgery no one told me. Children could not go into a hospital in those days, but I was so miserable that they snuck me in through a back door to see her. She was hooked up to all sorts of machinery, and to my child's eyes it all looked so terrible. Still, I got to see her. I guess she took a turn for the worse and was in the hospital for a long time.

Enjoying an ice cream. A rare treat with her mother due to tight finances.

My Dad (Stepdad – but I called him Dad because he was all I knew) didn't know what to do with me so he sent me to his friend's home. I did not know these people and all I did was cry. He finally took me to my cousin's house. It was not until my aunt told me about Mom, and that she was sick but would be okay, that I finally calmed down.

Eventually, my parents saved some money and sent me for two weeks to a camp for horseback riding. I was in Heaven. The first day we got to choose our horse and I got a magnificent palomino. We learned how to groom, bridle and saddle our horses. On the third day, one of the counselors took me aside, pushed me against the wall, and told me that I needed to tell the other counselors that I did not want the horse or he would beat me. I was so frightened and having no skill or understanding to even go and report him, I let him take my beautiful palomino. There were no other horses so I got some old nag who could hardly move. I remember sitting on that horse crying. Someone finally got me a better horse and asked why I gave mine up, but I was too afraid to say.

As I said in the beginning, I do not remember much about my early childhood, other than times that created emotion, either good or bad. I blocked out much of my life as a shield against that pain. By the time I got to high school I began to come out of my shell. I met the man who would eventually become my husband. Ralph and I were fast friends; we went to the movies, horseback riding, and archery shooting – just enjoying our time together and learning about trust and cooperation. He was, and remains, my best friend and supporter in all that I choose to do.

After graduation I started looking for work. My

Russian-born grandfather told me that I would be lucky to get a job out of high school paying more than $45 a week. At the time, that was considered a normal minimum wage for people just starting out. I got myself a job, and for $50 a week, and was so proud of myself for doing that. Soon after, Ralph encouraged me to apply for a job at General Motors, which I got at a whopping $55 a week plus overtime.

Grandparents in 1960.

In my family it was important for a woman to have a career, especially in light of my mother's circumstances. My stepfather was a podiatrist and felt that medicine was the best profession. My plan was to become a medical technician, spending most of my time in the lab and not with patients. I felt I would be too sensitive to patients' feelings and it was safer for me to be a bit removed from dealing with them directly.

I had applied to a school for medical technicians, but quickly realized the career path for technicians was better served with hands-on experience. So, I quit my job at General Motors even though by then I was earning $95 a week plus bonuses. I was certain I could find a position working in a lab, even though I had no experience and only a little college, which I was still attending at night.

I was equal parts foolish, hopeful, and steadfast. Yet I applied for and got a job at Women's Hospital in NYC, where I worked directly with the Pathologist, accessing data for pathological tissue studies.

On Saturdays, I would come in on my own time to learn how to process and cut representative sections from the surgeries that had been performed. Eventually, I was able to take a test to obtain a license as a histologist. Don't ask me how I passed this test. I studied from the Armed Forces Institute of Pathology manual and tried to assimilate knowledge that I had yet to experience firsthand. Years later, I began to work at Roosevelt Hospital Pathology Laboratory on 59th street in NYC. There they worked with more diverse tissues and special staining processes. I had only read about this in the manual but now I was actually doing this specialty work.

By the time I was twenty years old I had already worked three jobs in career fields and was getting ready to marry my high school sweetheart.

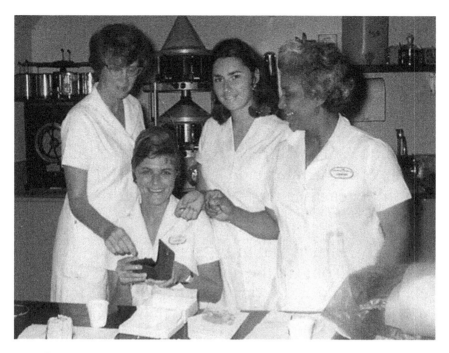

Ladies working at Roosevelt Hospital: Joan, Eva, Marilyn, and Joy.

Ralph and I were married in October 1963 and had two sons – Michael in 1969, and Steven in 1972. Six weeks after Steven was born, I joined a health club to lose weight. They offered a self-defense program for which I immediately signed up. Previously, I had started yoga and tennis, as well as adult education courses delving into some psychic ability, but nothing piqued my interest the way martial arts did. I loved the training.

"Dan" – our karate man – was actually teaching some Tae Kwon Do and self-defense. When they discontinued the program, I arranged for him to come to my home and teach. My best friend, Kathy, and I were trained in my living room, while four children ranging in ages from infant to six years old kept themselves busy. What I was discovering was an inner self I did not realize existed. Had this man discouraged me or pointed out how terrible I was, who knows if I would have pursued my training. When his schedule made it impossible for him to continue teaching us, I began to look for an actual dojo.

I quickly learned that in 1972, women were not exactly welcome in the dojo. I was offered the chance to take a self-defense program, but totally discouraged from joining actual martial arts programs.

After a number of unsuccessful ventures, I found a program at a local Jewish Center. Here again, I was told to take the women's self-defense course, but by then I knew I wanted more. It was finally decided that I could take the karate class – if I first took the self-defense class!

I was the first woman to be allowed in Jimmy Papa's class. There I began to learn about Okinawan Isshinryu Karate. Simultaneously I was delving deeper into energy work and was excited to see so much of it in my newly found karate training. Doors were opening to me mentally, spiritually, and physically...but it was not always a smooth sailing inside and outside the dojo.

Chapter 2 – Getting What I Wished For

Early in my life I had been content to do all the things I was supposed to do...yet something was always missing. During the day I could take care of the house and children, but in the evening I began my training in the hopes of gaining balance. I wanted to find path to my true self.

I need to admit right here that I was terrible at karate when I first started. I could not make a proper fist or stand on one leg to do a kick. However, what I lacked in talent I made up for with determination. All that mattered was that I had managed to find someone who would teach me at a time when everyone else was saying no. Jimmy had opened a new door for me.

One day a gentleman named Nick Adler came to our

class to show movies of Shimabuku Tatsuo (the founder of Isshinryu Karate) and discuss the forms as well as its history. This grabbed my interest. The methods of Isshinryu were starting to make sense to me, especially the vertical fist which felt strong to my light frame. Adler Sensei had my attention.

Nick Adler Sensei, a senior in Isshinryu Karate.

Unfortunately, that early meeting was not as warm and encouraging as I might have hoped. Adler Sensei spoke only to his black belt who led the dojo. We, the students, just listened as bystanders. When we were leaving I stopped and offered a respectful bow to say thank you for the presentation. He gave me a look as if I should not have spoken to him at all.

In 1974 when Jim stopped teaching I again looked for a local dojo. By then I enjoyed Isshinryu, and even though I was not very good at it, I had finally achieved my yellow belt. In Jim's absence I found a local school willing to accept women but it was a different style. Finally, I made the decision that if I wanted to stay with Isshinryu I needed to go to Adler Sensei's dojo, the man whom I did not like.

This was a difficult and soul-searching choice. I asked another student (David) who had been in Jim's class to come with me to the Bayshore dojo. At that time it was a two story walkup which later became three flights just to get to class.

At the time Adler Sensei had a teaching partner who was easier to talk to, so I figured I would just work with him and not speak to Sensei unless I had to.

David and I signed up for his class and I was immediately started at white belt once more.

Unbeknownst to me, David had tested at Adler Sensei's dojo, not only doing basics and forms but also Kumite (fighting), so his rank was accepted and mine was not. Adler Sensei was difficult...but fair. He had no problem with a woman in his class and in fact had promoted two women to black belt rank. The difference in his philosophy was that he treated all students in his class equally. He did not give the traditional striped belts for women and children at that time. He felt that if you earned a black belt it should be a true black belt.

Several months after joining the dojo the office manager left so I began to help out and even assist in classes. Nothing but the best was good enough for Sensei. I came to realize that I could not please him but instead had to try to be better every day.

It was less than a year after I joined that Sensei moved to the third floor of the building. We had to be in good condition just to navigate all those stairs with a full Gi bag. He had a giant floor heater that sounded like a jet engine which he would turn on in the winter but have to turn off so we could hear him. In the summer we had huge floor fans to cool the place down. One summer day when our attic dojo was already an oven Sensei decided to conduct tests. I was testing for one of my brown belt levels and had to perform all my Kata one after another where the bow out became the bow in to the next form.

About half way through the test my uniform was totally drenched and I was beginning to feel dizzy. I guess I did a little self talk and began to focus on one move at a time, telling myself to just keep moving. At the end I got promoted, and one of the students asked what would have happened if I had passed out. Sensei's response was, "She would have failed."

One day when he was teaching Adler Sensei did a stepover kick and a large knothole in the old wooden floor came out. I was quite impressed even though the feat was probably a symptom of old boards. He was about to throw it away when I asked if I could keep it. It was an odd request at the time, but he shrugged and handed it to me. Twenty years and several dojo later I was able to have that same piece mounted on a plaque with an Eagle (Adler means Eagle in German) and present it to him at his Northeastern Open Tournament which was held in September.

20 Years of training with my Sensei Master Nick Adler.

This is the Plaque I presented to him and what it said.

Master Nick Adler

MY TEACHER AND MY FRIEND

I'VE LEARNED FROM YOU IN MANY WAYS

YOU HAVE THE GIFT OF TEACHING,

YOU'VE SHARED WITH ME YOUR KNOWLEDGE

ALWAYS SENSED WHEN I WAS REACHING.

I FEEL THAT YOU'VE ENRICHED MY LIFE -

YOU'VE INFLUENCED MY THINKING,

YOU'VE LED ME INTO LEARNING

KEPT MY EAGERNESS FROM SHRINKING.

YOU'VE BROADENED ME WITH CHALLENGE.

ENTERTAINED ME WITH YOUR STYLE,

YOU'VE OPENED UP MY INTEREST

BY ELICITING A SMILE.

I'VE SENSED THE MANY MOMENTS

WHEN YOUR WIT AND WISDOM GLISTENED.

I'LL LONG RECALL THE TIMES

WHEN YOU HAVE TALKED AND I HAVE LISTENED.

WITH LOVE, RESPECT AND DEDICATION,

YOUR STUDENT

Marilyn

MARILYN FIERRO

SEPTEMBER 22, 1994

When I look back on those days now, I wonder how I managed to continue. There were no pads and my arms were so bruised after some of the classes that my husband asked me to wear long sleeves in public. I guess he didn't want curious eyes to think he was abusing me. I finally created arm pads out of some old socks and began to wear them. Everyone laughed at me in the dojo, but at least I could continue my training without fear of getting my husband arrested. I was still not up to the standards of the other students but each day I was getting a little better. All the while I saw the spiritual aspects of the art and knew one day it would come together for me.

Marilyn Fierro

Marilyn with Adler Sensei and "the boys". Fierro Sensei was always held to the same standards as the male students.

Chapter 3 – Growing Pains

The word "karate-ka" is wonderful. It does not mean a man, woman, or child, but a person who trains in karate. I resisted teaching women's self-defense programs and luckily Sensei did not make me teach only children. I was one of the guys and trained as hard as they did.

In traveling to various parts of the country for competition, I began to see an increase in the number of women competing. I was very encouraged by this. It was at the Isshinryu Hall of Fame in Tennessee when I saw a locker room filled with women competitors for the first time. This was sometime in the late 70s and since then I have seen the growth of women in the martial arts steadily increase.

In 1978, with Adler Sensei's encouragement, I began a karate program in Kings Park and by the end of that year Sensei and I opened the Smithtown Karate Academy near my home. I was able to receive my black belt several months after we opened that dojo. Within a year Sensei had opened a health club and dojo in Sayville and needed to be there full time. I found myself as the owner of the Smithtown Dojo.

I never wanted to be a dojo owner or a sensei. I only wanted to be a good martial artist and my Sensei's right hand person. I had put my heart and soul into the dojo - I could not close it and I was terrified to run it. Alone! How frightening it seemed at that time.

I began the difficult transition from student to teacher. I think I wanted to prove to Adler Sensei that I could do it. The first year was so very difficult and I did not know if I could make it. Most of the students already enrolled at Smithtown were Adler Sensei's students, so they naturally followed him to Sayville. When I felt close to quitting my husband stepped in and encouraged me to push on for a little longer. I also connected with Joyce Santamaria, the only other female dojo owner I knew, and she supported me during that first difficult year.

Fierro Sensei teaching at the original Smithtown Karate Academy

When I first took over the dojo there were many challenges, not just in teaching, but also with people who would come into the school to question what I was doing, poke fun at our Isshinryu punch, or to tell me that what I did would not work. Each time I was able to get these people to leave, and normally with an apology from them. I had to learn to handle these people in a confident manner without being physical with them. I was a non-Asian, female teacher in a male dominated art of Asian origin. When I took over the dojo the challenge was to remain who I am and not try to be someone else.

Everyone needs to find their own style of teaching, which for me was a balance between being tough and maintaining my own personality. My feminine side, you might say. Naturally, it took years for that to happen but eventually it all came into focus for me.

Difficulties as a female teacher in karate extended beyond the dojo as well. The men in my group of friends would grab me at odd times and ask, "What are you gonna do about this?" They knew I was training in the martial arts and, of course, they thought a woman had no place in that world. They might have even thought they were doing me a favor, showing me that my training could never save me from a man's strength.

My response to these situations – at first – was nothing, because at my core I was still a nice person who didn't want to hurt a fly. When hearing about these encounters, Adler Sensei pointed out that these men were being disrespectful to me and I should not allow that to happen.

The next time we were at a party and someone started to grab me from behind they got elbowed in the gut, and before I had a chance to finish the rest of my move they folded up. "Why did you do that?", they would ask. I would simply say, "You should not be touching me."

That was the last time someone in my group of friends tried to play games.

On one occasion a 4th dan student of mine, John Bolton, attended an Isshinryu seminar by Ed McGrath Hanshi. He really impressed McGrath Hanshi, who then asked John about his instructors. John said he studied with me, and McGrath immediately corrected him by saying, "You mean Nick Adler don't you?" John said, "No, I train under Fierro Sensei."

McGrath later went on to ask Adler Sensei if John was his student. Of course, Sensei stated clearly that John was with me.

Another student of mine named Chris went to college and met an instructor who was surprised that Chris was training with a woman. Chris hadn't really considered it unusual until he had been questioned about it that day.

When I first started training I had the rather audacious goal of trying to achieve brown belt. But once I got there, I found the confidence to keep going all the way. This is what martial arts training did for me. I took each day as it came, and tried to get a little better one step at a time.

The benefits of martial arts training are unlimited and with the changing times there is a place for everyone. Every participant will take what they can from their training and be better because of it. Then again, not everyone can stick with the discipline and lifestyle that transform you, body and mind.

The following is a saying that I saw in Adler Sensei's dojo and from time to time in publications. In my experience, the numbers ring true.

For every 10,000 students that join a karate class, half will drop out the first month.

Of that 5,000 one half will remain the second month.

Of the remaining students 1,00 will complete six months of training and then quit.

500 Will study for a year, but only 100 will see their second anniversary.

Three will make first degree black belt, but only one will go on to teach others what is to be learned.

For karate is now part of this person's life and they shall go on to share this life with others.

THIS PERSON IS A SENSEI

"Think about it, she's one in ten thousand." – Spoken by my sister-in-law.

Marilyn Fierro

Chapter 4 – Growth Through Competition

I have two regrets in regards to karate. The first and foremost is that Shimabuku Tatsuo Soke passed in 1975 when I was beginning this journey and I never had the chance to meet him. The second is that I never kept a karate journal to help me be accurate as I share my experiences. So if I am disjointed or gloss over dates I ask for your indulgence and suggest you, the reader, learn from my mistakes. If something is important to you, keep track, write it down, and journal about it.

As I trained harder, taught, and competed, I began to understand my forms far better than ever before. I also began to feel accepted not just as a woman in the martial arts but as someone pioneering in uncharted territory.

The first tournament I remember participating in was the 1976 "A Tribute to a Master" in Queens, New York. It was a special event to honor the first anniversary of the passing of our founder, Shimabuku Tatsuo Sensei. Master Shimabuku was one of the world's leading Okinawan karate masters, and a legend in his time.

Because of the scarcity of female competitors there was only one division for women, white to black belt. Naturally, women like myself who had less experience were at a disadvantage going up against the black belts. One woman, Maria Melendez, was a higher ranked black belt and far more qualified than anyone else. She fought for and gained the right to do forms with the men.

I wanted so much to please Adler Sensei in those tournament years, and tried so hard to win each time I competed. One day he pulled me aside and said to me, "You don't win for me. Be your best for yourself." That one statement changed everything for me.

From that moment on I simply tried to get a better score each time I competed in kata or weapons. My goals changed. I wasn't trying to gain favor in someone else's eyes anymore. I was trying to make myself better...for me. Eventually I saw the results and I began to win trophies, but more than that I won by conquering something within myself.

As the years passed, more and more women became involved in the martial arts and entered tournaments. Adler Sensei was one of the first tournament promoters to offer separate women's divisions and separate bouts for rank levels. I also believe they were the first to offer a Woman's Grand Champion. He was always fair to us. I competed against people like Kathy (Baxter) Loukopoulos in AAU who went on to become a World Champion, and Cynthia Rothrock who was a frequent East Coast competitor.

Cynthia was an awesome, energetic Kung Fu competitor. So was Christine Bannon Rodrigues. They both eventually became movie stars thanks to their talents and remained good friends of mine.

Fierro Sensei with Cynthia Rothrock

Adler Sensei took us everywhere to compete. My

first trophy was at Errol Bennett's tournament in the Bronx. It was a difficult division and I was beyond pleased with the results. You can imagine the shock on my face when my name was announced. I wasn't used to winning anything; I just tried my best. My emphasis had always been on self-defense and the moves necessary for the street.

Fierro Sensei during an intense tournament performance

In 1981 I competed in the Metropolitan AAU Championships sponsored by Terry Maccarrone Sensei. A reporter from Newsday named Joe Krupinski was at the event. We spoke for a while and he came back to me several times. I told my Sensei that I was sure I would be in the story because he kept asking me about the philosophy of the martial arts even more than the skill and competition. When the story came out My name was the first in the article and Mister Krupinski referred to me again ending it with me as well. I believe he was the first to really grasp what it was I had been trying to say about martial arts and the connection between the physical and spiritual. He titled his article "The Sport/Religion of Karate".

By 1982 I had yet to win first place in the male black belt weapons division, which was a rather ambitious goal of mine. I struggled against far better competitors and the stigma of women performing in a "man's sport" but I was determined to make it happen. I had already begun fulfilling the criteria for my Sandan level. This is the third degree Dan ranking, at which level a student is expected to be able to train other students on their own. My criteria was simple: I owned a dojo and a separate karate program, and I even had a two page story printed about me in Taekwondo times. But my final criteria was that I needed to win first place with my tonfa.

The Tonfa is a handle on a rice grinder in Okinawa. Because it was set in concrete it could easily break so farmers kept several spare around making it easy to grab one for self defense if needed. While it is similar to a police baton is more efficient as a blocking, striking and wielding weapon. Note Tonfa are also called Teefa or Chiefa and are used in pairs!

Master Don Nagle's tournament. I was going against competitors of far higher rank and experience. On the drive up to the event I had explained my criteria and plan to Adler Sensei. He misinterpreted me and thought I was asking for a promotion. We had a heated exchange which left me angry throughout the day. That fire worked to my advantage.

I performed my tonfa kata with precision and passion. My scores reflected the effort and were good enough to grant me first place. It was a tiny trophy, but remains my favorite to this day.

That evening at an after tournament gathering

hosted by Master Nagle, Adler Sensei promoted me to Sandan and Master Nagle gave me a big hug saying how I deserved the promotion. Two people I admired the most had just helped me to fulfill the second goal I had in karate – what a special and memorable moment!

Fierro Sensei celebrating her first 1st Place win in the Black Belt Men's Kobudo Division

One day at Don Nagle's tournament I had been judging for a while and eventually took a lunch break I went to get a sandwich and Master Isaac Henry of Beikoku Karate-Do Gojukai (BKG) was sitting there and invited me to join him. I have no idea how the conversation went into the energy of martial arts but eventually I mentioned Johnathan Livingston Seagull and we both were able to relate to it. As you know eventually he became an integral part of my story and first article.

I loved competing when Master Steve Armstrong and Master Lou Lizotte had the American Okinawan Karate Association events in Connecticut. They were always at a hotel ballroom and I would pray to have a ring that was on carpet. My dojo was carpeted so that made it easy to relax my mind and feel like I was at home. Also, most people trained on wood or Tatami floors and could not get used to the carpet. I always seemed to win when I went to those events.

I did forms with the women but competed against men in the weapons divisions. Master Lizotte, who I just mentioned, is a strict no-nonsense kind of man and I had a lot of respect for him although he could be difficult to work with. At least you knew what you were in for with him, in retrospect a lot like my own Sensei. He surprised me by making me a center referee for men's black belt divisions.

In those earlier days a center referee was the place to be. Personally I would rather be an excellent corner ref and support for the center referee than to take on the responsibility that centering entails. As an official in any capacity I tend to be very strict especially about forms, which to me are the backbone of any martial arts style. I also believe in honesty and, if asked, will explain my scoring in detail (even if that means pointing out faults).

Fierro Sensei with Lou Lizotte, a tough but fair tournament operator.

Charles Rice, Jr and Melvin Early from Detroit were some of the toughest fighters I know. I used to feel they hated me because I was so strict on them. They seemed to invariably end up in my corner. It could just be coincidence but I do know some competitors who did just that. It is only recently when we spoke they have told me I was wrong and they have always respected me. Honestly I never knew that.

I should mention that I competed once with a bo. The Bo is a long staff weapon made for blocking, striking, and sweeping. It is definitely not my weapon of choice. In fact, a certain instructor from New Jersey told me never to try it again. Ever. So, I stuck with my tonfa since I truly love that weapon.

Challenging yourself is a must in martial arts, and in life, but sometimes you need to know where your limitations are.

The Second World Championships for the Isshinryu World Karate Association and the first in the United States with Shimabuku Kichiro O' Sensei was held at Brookdale Community College in New Jersey. Adler Sensei's daughter was getting married around that time and the dress rehearsal was the day of the tournament. So, Adler Sensei arranged for his Sensei, Master Don Nagle, to bring me to the tournament.

My Sensei's Sensei (say that five times fast!) was responsible for me and I once again wanted to be perfect. I forgot my Sensei's advice, and my own rule – never to compete for the approval of others, only for the betterment of myself.

I was competing with Chinto Kata. Adler Sensei had recently changed the way we performed the opening sequence and when we got to the tournament I practiced and practiced. I was focused on pleasing Nagle Sensei the whole time. Eventually my name was called and I went up to perform. As soon as I began my Kata I reverted to the old opening series, and when I realized there was no way to fix it I simply stopped. I turned to the judges and bowed out of the ring. It was all I could do to keep from bursting into tears before the division was over and the second I could escape I ran to the ladies room to cry.

I was just so frustrated at myself. People stopped me later to ask what had happened. They saw the opening of the kata and couldn't understand why I stopped. No one even noticed my error! I had stopped for nothing because I wanted to look good for one of my teachers. Nagle, of course never let me forget my true mistake. Martial arts is done to improve the individual. Not for anyone else's glory or respect.

A year or so later Master Nagle had his Kampai (Cheers!) Party and that year included women. I attended, of course, but there were no female black belts so I just sat at the table with the women. At a Kampai Party the guys sit on the floor and each one makes a toast and everyone drinks to it.

After the toast went around the room once Master Nagle said, "There is someone here who's earned the right to speak because she knows what it's like to try and fail but survive to fight another day." He nodded at me.

After that party I sent him my photo from the failed competition, with the correct opening move of Chinto.

Fierro Sensei enjoying time with Don Nagle and Nick Adler

Several months later I had the opportunity to compete in Master Willie Adams tournament in Detroit. Prior to that my knee had been popping in and out when I was practicing Chinto so I planned to perform Seiuchin kata instead. Seiuchin is a unique kata and very useful for someone having leg or knee issues since only hand and arm movements are used.

As I lined up to compete I noticed Master Nagle as the center referee. Remembering that embarrassing moment at Brookdale Community College I knew this was a rare chance to redeem myself. All I could do was pray that I could do the double jump kick and land without my knee going out.

I held my breath and concentrated on doing the best I could just for me, and I performed each move one at a time. It worked, and I was so happy. The fact that I won first place was icing on the cake.

I would go with Adler Sensei on occasion to Nagle's Jersey City Dojo but never trained there. I did absorb a lot by watching and listening. Sometimes Master Adler would teach the class and Nagle and I would talk. He would tell me to call him Don and I would say okay Sensei but never really did. It just felt too disrespectful.

One time he told me a story about when he was a kid in school and the other kids had been picking on him. I guess Master Nagle was always smart but not always the fighter we know him as today. So he hide rocks behind all the trees on the way home and when he was chased by the bullies he would run from tree to tree and throw rocks at them. He planned ahead, and he was ready to defend himself. Of course, the Don Nagle who was the first American to win an Okinawan Championship as a white belt and thus earned his black belt was no longer the same kid. He was a well respected Jersey City Police officer and revered martial artist. Don Nagle passed on August 23, 1999. It remains difficult for my Sensei to have lost his teacher and I too miss our talks and his easy wisdom.

A mentor, legend, and friend.

I became a 6th Dan in March of 1994. In America, 6th Dan wears a red with white belt, but we were going by Okinawan standards so I had to wait until 7th to get those colors. We went to Connecticut for an AOKA tournament where Maria Melendez, a competitor in the 1976 Tribute to a Master tournament, was promoted to 6th Dan. She told me she was the highest woman there and I told her I was already 6th. She asked me, "Well where's your red with white obi?" Pictures were taken with all the masters and I was out because I did not have that belt.

Being excluded from that photo simply because I didn't have the right color belt stung, but I kept it bottled inside. Soon after, Adler Sensei presented me with a beautiful Shureido red with white belt to wear only at American events. He said he never wanted that to happen to me again.

Fierro Sensei receiving her red and white belt.

One time my dojo brother, Tommy May, had a tournament in a park in New Rochelle. The single competition area was a boxing ring set up in the park. I was competing with Chatan Yara no Sai. By the time it was my turn the ring was in full sun and burning hot. We had to dip our feet in water before entering the ring to keep from being scalded, which made it slippery. I was a bit nervous about slipping so was being cautious with my form, but as I progressed there was one part of the kata where the left foot stays in one place while the right one moves in and out. My left foot started burning on the hot surface of the ring so instead of completing Chatan Yara I went right into Kusanku Sai to end the form quickly. I didn't even wait for my scores before exiting the ring and soaking my feet once more. I got second place for Chatan Yara no Kusanku Sai Kata and a blister on my foot.

Rick Adler, Kevin Nentwich, and I traveled to Indianapolis, Indiana for the Isshinryu World Karate Association World Championships. There I competed with my tonfa yet again. All the men were competing with bo. I thought I did my best tonfa kata ever and received a wonderful ovation from the crowd. Then I went to check my scores only to find they were very low. So I went to speak to the judges. They asked me where I learned the form I had used. I explained it to them because as it turned out, they were unfamiliar with it. In retrospect, I should have asked why they scored me so low simply because they did not know my kata. It was a different time in the evolution of tournaments I guess and I was not one to argue. At least not then. Many people told me later that they were shocked I did not even place. It seemed the edge always went to the competitors the judges already knew.

I used to compete at the Isshinryu Hall of Fame (IHOF) in Tennessee and always did very well there. But in 1986 I had some major abdominal surgery and I don't think I ever got my competition momentum back. The first time I competed with my tonfa after being sick was at the IHOF. They had nine judges for the black belt weapons competitions. All of them were red, or red and white belts. Many of the competitors were intimidated by that high ranking board and many good competitors made errors just from being psyched out. I was not intimidated, but it wasn't because of some inner peace I had gained. I was actually relaxed figuring I had no chance anyway.

I began my form and just a couple of moves in my tonfa got caught under my sleeve after a punch. I could not manage to gracefully get it out so I bowed out of the form. Thankfully, at that event black belts were allowed to restart. They asked me to try again, but I said "no" since I was a black belt and my gaffe would have resulted in death in real combat. Adler Sensei was sitting in the center and he said through clenched teeth, "Do it again." Well. You don't argue in a situation like that.

I started over and this time it came out really good. Later Adler Sensei said if I had done it that way the first time I would have won.

I competed just a little while longer before deciding

it was best to focus more on my teaching and develop my refereeing skills. I totally admire those who are both excellent competitors, teachers and referees for it is quite difficult to do it all.

I learned to referee in both AAU and USANKF events. International rules are difficult to learn and it takes a lot of time and commitment not to mention the expense of memberships and travel to fulfill those obligations. I am glad I did it because Sensei and I had an opportunity to travel to Venezuela thanks to Sensei Javier Martinez. Although there was a language barrier we were able to work as a unit in our divisions because Japanese terminology and judging hand signals are universal.

The first plaque I received for Judging was from Master Tom La Puppet, Shotokan Karate , who was in charge of the Metropolitan AAU. I never expected any recognition so that came as a most welcome surprise. As the years went by I received many such awards but I always remember that very first one.

In July 2003 I attended the KIAI Grand Nationals in Reno and was asked if I wanted to perform on stage in the Masters demonstrations. I decided to challenge myself by participating. I am a teacher at heart and can lead a lesson at the drop of a hat...but performing on a stage? That is a different story all-together.

What I did not know was that there was going to be mirrors behind me, a screen in front of me, and Taiko Drummers beating a rhythm while the masters performed! Quite the spectacle. I think my heart was pounding with the drummers as I awaited my turn to perform my favorite kata, Hamahiga no Tonfa. My name was announced and I entered the stage taking a spot in the middle. I bowed and announced my form and began to move. The drummers began to beat. It all seemed to be going so fast so I told myself to slow it down a bit. In front of me was a large screen and I could see myself as well as the audience but I tried to remain focused as I turned around...and that was when I noticed the mirrors on the back wall.

Now I could see myself coming and going with the screen reflecting in the mirror. I have that video clip on my web page because it continues to take my breath away. To see that many of yourself while you're trying to concentrate on making your legs go this way and your arms go that way...well, it took all I had to get through that demonstration. But afterward, at the banquet I walked into the room to applause. I was confused until my friend and fellow competitor, Ray Gabriel, pointed behind me and I turned to see me, doing Hamahiga on the big screen at the head of the room.

Apparently I did well enough to impress my friends.

So many people come into our lives we never meet again or do not remember at all. Sometimes a person will come up to me to say they saw a news article which I was in or caught one of my Public Access TV shows. Those times make me understand that who we are often reaches further than we think.

Take the time when I was first starting out on my own with a dojo. Sensei Joyce Santamaria had a junior tournament at the mall. She asked me to officiate at it and I said yes. Fast forward from that moment about ten years later and I found myself at the same mall, shopping. A young man stopped me to say he recognized me from his first tournament, the very same one I officiated for Santamaria Sensei. Not only did he remember me, but he proceeded to take out his wallet and pull out a photo of my much younger self. Somehow I had impressed him so much that he had carried that photo with him all this time.

When you're a judge at the tournament level you see a variety of techniques and styles. I once saw a man competing at one of Master Chuck Merriman's tournaments who was using Monkey Style Kung Fu, and he was excellent at it. At the time I remember thinking to myself that I was glad not to be a judge for him because I was laughing at the performance till tears were flowing. Luckily Adler Sensei had seen him in the past so he and the other judges were able to remain professional.

Here is where fate can be a funny thing. Much, much later I was center referee for men's lightweight black belt fighting and there he was. This same man was in that division and was so fast with his reverse punch no one could avoid him. It was good to see his speed and agility in action that day and it sure taught me a lesson about judging someone from a first impression.

Over my years of involvement in the martial arts I have trained and received judging certification in both the Amateur Athletic Union (AAU) and the USA Nataional Karate-do Federation (USANKF). NKF was by far the more difficult and strict of the two. That was fine because it often produced a high quality official. One time, maybe in the early 90s, Adler Sensei and I went to the NKF Nationals in Texas. I had studied hard for the written exam. For the practical I was one of the corner judges. A roundhouse kick came that was more to the other side but at the angle I was seated I could see it touch. However, Davy Crocket, the instructor at the time, was in a different position and he questioned my call. He made a big showing of how my angle was wrong and I could not possibly see the technique hit. It was quite embarrassing, but because I was going for certification I kept my mouth shut. Afterwards people sitting near me said they too saw the technique. Given who I am today I believe I would have handled that differently, like asking him to sit and have the fighters reenact the kick, but I didn't...so that was that.

The next day at the tournament I was again a side judge. We were given a short break for lunch which was Mexican food and not sitting well at all and later there was a short five minute break if you needed the bathroom. The men's room was close but the ladies much further away. I finally said to the Chief Referee, "Look, I do not go to the bathroom, unzip my pants, whip it out, shake it and put it back and leave without washing my hands. I need more time."

He looked a bit shocked and said, "...Okay, take as long as you need."

During the training Mr. Crocket emphasized the importance of unity and backing up the center referee. So, if the chief referee asks for a reconsideration from you then you should change your vote to be supportive. Later that same day he substituted his top female student to be center referee in my ring. When "Yame" (stop) was called and we were to call the point I raised my flag for what I clearly saw.

I do not remember if I was a lone caller for that technique or not, but she looked at me and made the sign for reconsideration. I did not call the other point I just switched to a no see since I had already called what I did see. She was only in my ring for that one bout.

The event ran really late and we could not stay much longer so we went to him to get our judging booklets and grades. He asked me why I changed my call when I was asked and I told him because he had said at the meeting to support your center referee no matter what. The bottom line was both Adler Sensei and myself were told we were lucky because we could keep our officiating level but 90% were going to be dropped down. Shocking to say the least. We had spent all that money to fly to Texas, pay for hotel and food as well as the cost of the seminar and certification only to keep what we already had and to be treated like naughty children. I never had a desire to return to those events in the future.

I have judged at large events like the Arnold Classic in Ohio and all of the major Isshinryu events without ever feeling that way again. I even officiated at some of the Atlantic Oil Team events when they were on the east coast. The pressure there was immense as there was a lot of money at stake for the competitors so you do not want to be the judge to make a wrong call.

As the years wore on I began to accumulate awards as an official which to me were as special if not more so than the trophies I had earned as a competitor. I don't necessarily need the shiny statues or the plaques to validate what I've done, but in a way it makes me feel good to know that I've done things the right way and people have noticed. The trophies exist as tangible proof that I really have come as far as I think I have.

Recently at the 2016 OIKKA World Championships in New Jersey we ran our ring almost non-stop from 10 am until 5:30. Master Reese Rigby was the center referee and I, along with Master Carl Martin, Renshi Scott LaPelusa and a gentleman I had just met were the corner officials. I have to say we had one of the smoothest running rings at the event. Our kata scores were right on and if they deviated it was merely one tenth of a point difference. We ran several of the Grand Champion divisions and were the last ring running with so many events. The next morning at the hotel I will filling a juice cup when I heard a small voice behind me say, "Hello." I turned and there was a young boy who told me I was one of judges in his ring. I asked him if I did a good job and he said "...yes," then I asked if he had won and he said, "YES!" I thought it was adorable that he wanted to tell me that.

I guess we will always be remembered in a good way by the winners. But, I hope I will be remembered by many as someone who cared enough to help them when they needed it and in some small way made a difference in their lives.

Life is full of such challenges, some that we inadvertently set up for ourselves and others that seem to come along from nowhere. It is how we face those challenges and what we take away from them that defines us in the end.

As Ralph Waldo Emerson's poem says: "To know even one life has breathed easier because you have lived, that is to have succeeded."

To laugh often and much

To win the respect

Of intelligent people

And the affection of children;

To earn the appreciation

Of honest critics and endure

The betrayal of false friends;

To appreciate beauty,

To find the best in others;

To leave the world

A bit better, whether

By a healthy child,

A garden patch

Or a redeemed social condition;

To know even one life

Has breathed easier

Because you have lived

That is to have succeeded.

- Ralph Waldo Emerson

Chapter 5 – My Sensei, Nick Adler

Most folks know my Sensei as a hardnosed old-school martial artist, which of course he is. But he is also a kind, fair, and honest person. With him, respect is something to be earned, not by what you say you can do, but by who you are when you are called upon to act.

Sensei walks his talk, as they say. I know there are probably as many people who do not like him as there are those who honor him for his actions and all he has done. Either way, everyone respects him. That is the value of a true warrior.

Adler Sensei during a relaxed tournament moment in 1985

Sensei never gave compliments. Although he has mellowed somewhat with age he is still the same man he always was. Tough as steel, able to bend like a reed, and more capable than any ten other men I know. When I was competing, I was not a winner unless I won first place. Not just because I was a woman who had to prove I could do everything as well as a man, but because that's the way it was.

There is only one winner in the end. It was a tough idea to follow but one that also made me far stronger than I thought I could be.

It's different today. Everyone who participates is given something that makes them feel like a "winner." Although I applaud the idea of encouraging people to do better and work harder – especially young people – I think the idea of making someone earn what they are given is something my Sensei would truly agree with.

I have a certificate on my wall for Nidan that was written on a brown paper bag. Occasionally someone will notice it and ask about it. I tell them it is a lesson in humility. When I was promoted to Nidan we were out of certificates and I asked Sensei when we would get them. His response to my disrespectful question was to say, "If I were to sign my name on a brown paper bag that should be enough." He was so right, because I was so wrong to even ask. That night I went home and wrote a certificate on a brown paper bag, and brought it back the next day for him to sign which he did without reservation. I'd earned it, but expecting a trophy to represent my accomplishments was selfish. When we finally did get certificates he asked me if I would take down the paper bag. I told him never. To this day that brown paper bag Nidan certificate holds a place of honor and reminder on my wall right next to my 9th Dan.

Lesson learned.

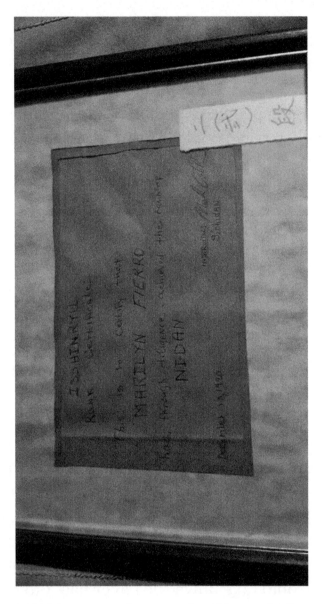

Adler Sensei is a man in search of knowledge. Not just in his early days, but even now. Sensei has an excellent memory and an analytical mind. He is quite visual and picks up even the slightest nuance in a move. No matter how hard I try there is no way I can achieve that skill level. His mind is so far ahead that he sometimes wonders why people do not immediately grasp what he already knows.

The passing of Grandmaster Don Nagle – Sensei's Sensei – in 1999 was a terrible blow to everyone involved with Isshinryu, to Sensei and to myself as well. To lose one's Sensei is like losing a parent.

There is a love and special relationship between sensei and student that anyone who has experienced can understand. The sensei is someone who brings us to maturity in the martial arts and, like a parent, is there to help and support us along the way. Don Nagle had been a good parent to Adler Sensei by supporting his growth as both a practitioner of the martial arts and as a person. Master Nagle did not stop sensei from growing and experimenting, and to his grandchild – me – he was every bit as caring and nurturing.

Grandmaster Nagle promoted Adler Sensei to 9th Dan in November 1995. In January 1996 he came to our camp and brought a video camera. He said he wanted to film this reenactment of Sensei's promotion so everyone would know about it. When he announced it once again to all who attended our winter camp that year he said, "When you are running in a relay you want to pass the torch to someone you know will carry it."

In August 1999, when Master Nagle passed, we went to New Jersey for the first day of his wake. I still remember seeing him there, laid out for viewing by those who had come to honor him. There was nothing to indicate his place as a pioneer for Isshinryu Karate. He was dressed in his Federal Marshall suit, which represented his occupation since retirement from the Jersey City Police force. It upset both Sensei and myself that karate, so much a part of his life, was being ignored.

When we returned home I immediately took out a photo of him, which he had previously sent to me, and had it enlarged and framed for the next day's viewing.

There were moments that second day at the wake when my heart was breaking and I had to leave the room to cry. In those moments many people walked up to me and asked if I was part of the family. I would say no, just a very close friend. I suppose, if I'd thought about it, I would have told them that yes, I was family. I was as much a part of his family as Adler Sensei, and others that Grandmaster Don Nagle had taken into his circle of instruction.

What the karate world admired in this awesome,

tough-as-nails person, was easy to see. He is often missed. He is often thought of. He is often quoted and emulated even now. He was a kind and caring man who looked out for everyone. At least that's how I also saw him, my friend with a kind heart.

Grandmaster Peter Urban, of Gojuryu Karate, was at the wake that next day when I brought in the enlarged photo. He brought a white lilly to place in the casket as a representation of the fallen warrior. Master Urban sat in the front of the room up near the casket. He seemed so alone. No one came up to him after he seated himself. It broke my heart to see him like that and so unlike the man that I knew.

I walked up to him and knelt down to tell him I know how sad it is for him to lose his friend. He told me, "It's over. This is the end of an era and there's no one left. He was the last." I told him not to say that. After all, he was still with us.

He told me that his spirit was already gone. All that was left was his shell.

The torch had been passed to the newer generation. People like Adler Sensei and myself. The older generation was passing away, and it was up to us to carry on the traditions.

In 2007, Adler Sensei brought Bobby Roeder and I to California to work with him on his *Insights into Okinawan Kobudo* series with Empire Media. We had a really good time but Sensei and I fought a lot as I tend to be quite critical of, well, everything. I want everything to be perfect so I would correct one thing and then another after a scene had been shot.

Finally Val Mijailovic, our videographer, just told me to say something as soon as I saw it. Sometimes it was as simple as a Gi not sitting correctly and at others it was basic mistakes one can make being on camera. Looking directly at the camera, trying to put your "good side" forward, that sort of thing. Regardless, I was the bad guy for a bit but in the end three wonderful DVD's were created and I even earned directorial credit.

One of the highlights of the trip was a visit to Val's Sensei, Takayuki Kubota. To give you an idea of how important Kubota Sensei is, he is the man who created a self-defense weapon still used today. A kubotan is a small, hard rod about the size of a pen meant to be carried on a keychain and held in your hand for defense when needed. Such a simple thing, developed by one of karate's great masters.

He was quite cordial to us and when Bobby worked out in his class he saw what a "Centurion" – our association – looked like. He was very pleased and most respectful to Sensei. I especially enjoyed learning about his meditation and the spiritual group his wife lead. Having used the Kubotan self-defense tool in my classes for a long time, it was an honor to meet its creator.

A reunion of old friends in 2007, from left to right: Bobby, Val, Kubota, Nick, Marilyn

It was karma that brought me to Adler Sensei's dojo and a miracle that those early days did nothing to dissuade my motivation or spirit. Fate took my hand and brought me to his door and I am blessed beyond measure for all the benefits I have gained. My life is different and so much better because a man I didn't initially even like became my mentor and friend. From Adler Sensei, among a wide variety of other things, I have learned this: never judge, always be open and understanding.

Chapter 6 – Being on Target

I love to tell the story of the time that I threw a peanut to an elephant at a circus and hit a man standing to my left. That of course was during my pre-karate days. Today I realize it was a problem of aim, release, and hand-eye coordination. At that time, however, I simply labeled myself as one who could not throw.

Training in karate taught me to have greater focus and concentration, but more so, it taught me how to set a goal and climb the obstacles in the way. It is not that I am always accurate, but that I have developed the skills necessary to adjust. "We cannot change the wind, but we can adjust our sails," as the saying goes. The idea is to recognize when we are off course and make the necessary corrections.

Change is difficult for everyone (and I am on the top of the list). Certainly Hanshi Adler can tell you how resistant to change I can be. But once I understand the reason I will quickly adapt. I have found that by changing my focus and direction from time to time great discoveries are possible. Often I will ask a student to throw a punch with the idea of demonstrating one self-defense technique only to find myself going into a totally different defense due to the energy, power, and angle being fed to me. Through training we learn to adjust rapidly as if our lives depend on it.

There is a thing I call the "twenty-year mark". Somewhere around that time all the training kicks in and with no thought at all we begin to react in exactly the correct manner for the situation we are presented with. I remember asking my Sensei over and over how he knew which technique to use and why we have so many defenses for a single attack. The answer was of course to keep training and I would come to understand.

Finally it did come, the moment when, with no thought, I could change to the appropriate defense as it was needed. I kept training, and I understood.

I was with a group of students at Suffolk Community College once, giving a demonstration. When I was done one of these students came up to ask a question. As he began his question his hands came toward me. I automatically saw a grab and used a circular move from Sanchin Kata to wrap his arms and push him away. I did this without thinking. It just came naturally. The student didn't take it in the same stride that I had, and he asked me why I would do that to him. I told him to ask his question but keep his hands to himself.

It is not a simple thing to teach reaction timing to a given situation. Instead, we teach a variety of defenses for different attacks to gain confidence and so one day they will know automatically what to do. This was the answer to the student's question, but I had demonstrated it more keenly with my actions than any amount of words would allow him to see.

I also believe that kata has the answers to most situations and practicing good kata will develop the skills for self-defense automatically.

I can still hear that man so many years ago asking me why I hit him with the peanut. If I had not begun this incredible journey into the martial arts I would still be that crazy lady trying to explain why I hit a man who was nowhere near my target. If we do not continue to grow where will we be in the next ten or twenty years? Exactly in the same position as we are today only ten to twenty years older. I, for one, believe that life is a journey and we might as well make it the most exciting and worthwhile experience ever.

"The only limit to our realization of tomorrow

will be our doubts of today."

Franklin Delano Roosevelt

Marilyn Fierro

Chapter 7 – Developing a Self-Defense Program

Years ago the thought of teaching a self-defense program to women would make me cringe. After all, I had spent years demanding to know why I should have to take a self-defense program when what I really wanted to do was learn martial arts.

Now I teach self-defense for women, but it has taken me a while to get the hang of it. I never seemed to be able to encourage the kind of intensity necessary for them to walk away from the program with a true concept of what it would take to defend themselves should the need arise.

From time to time I would be forced into teaching a group of women and found myself asking the big, controversial question, "are we simply nurturing a false sense of security?" I did not want to be guilty of causing more harm than good. The fact was that in the late 70s and early 80s women seemed more concerned about breaking a nail than learning a technique.

In truth, there was (and is) a real need for effective defense programs that empower the non-martial artist with usable tools for self-defense. Therefore I had to rethink the process from a perspective of the old me – the me before I discovered karate. What made me break through that layer of doubt and malaise, ignoring the advice of those around me that serious training wasn't my place?

As my martial arts progressed from white belt to green so too did my confidence grow. I remember standing in line to see a movie with my children when two teens standing in front of us started acting up and disturbing the group. I asked them to stop and one turned to me and said, "So make me." I replied, "Okay, fine." and with just my confidence and a single step the teens decided they didn't want to challenge me after all. That was interesting.

Another time I showed up at the dojo and the television was on, showing Muhammad Ali boxing. I had no interest so I left. I walked passed a bar that was located next door to the dojo on my way to my car. Upon getting close to the car I noticed a man in the parking lot with a golf club in his hand. He was an extremely tall man with flaming red hair drawn back into a ponytail. I saw him approach so I quickly opened my car door, threw everything in, and closed the door, keeping a short stick that I just learned to use in my hand.

I turned to face him as he approached with the golf club now over his shoulder. I don't know what his intentions were. All I know is that when I stood there and flipped the stick up into my hand, ready to meet his approach and do whatever I needed to in order to protect myself, he backed away and put the club down. He then proceeded to introduced himself. And we talked for a few minutes. Then he left. I was learning a valuable lesson to have confidence and not to back down.

There were other incidents in my life and as the years progressed I understood that the most powerful tool I had was ownership of my own self-worth. Once I understood that, no one could take that from me.

Today I start all of my programs by getting the women angry at the injustice of becoming a victim. I show them what it means to take control of their lives and I provide the facts and training to back it up.

Fierro Sensei posing after a successful Women's Self-Defense seminar

In 1978 I participated as part of a joint team with Police Officers and educators to inform women of the risks they face on a daily basis. We were there to give the people in the classes all the obvious statements about a buddy system and keeping yourself safe and so on. But when the police began to speak they said it is better to give in to rape rather than fight back and risk being killed.

Shocking. This was actually the prevailing theory back in the 1970s. The concern was for the woman's life, of course, but in essence they were saying, "Let yourself be a victim." I, of course, did not believe that anyone should just "let it happen" so instead I spoke more about avoidance and not letting yourself get put in that situation in the first place.

For any woman who has been raped, or assaulted, or abused, they understand that when it ends, it is not over. It stays with them for a lifetime. Passivity was not an answer.

I needed to let women know they had to *act*. They had to defend themselves. If I wanted to help women to protect themselves, I needed to make them angry. Not just upset that the system wasn't treating them fairly but angry enough to take steps in their own defense. Thus started my quest to provide the perfect program. One that was very different than others available to women at the time.

Awareness is the key to success! In self-defense programs it means avoidance of problems before they begin, and in life it is recognizing an opportunity and seizing it before the moment passes.

Now, as much as it got under my skin in my earlier years that I was only allowed to take self-defense classes, I now see that for some people a class in self-defense is the perfect way to develop confidence, and awareness. The hope was that the classes would trigger at the least a desire to take control of one's life and maybe even spark a desire to pursue Martial Arts for life.

Those of us who instruct self-defense often refer to these classes as "danger avoidance." Nobody can walk around prepared for a fight all the time. Nor should we go looking for one. We can, however, carry ourselves with assurance and confidence. In a research program conducted in the 1970s, prisoners who were incarcerated for mugging people were asked to view tapes of people walking down the street. They were then asked to pick out their potential victims. They chose their targets based on the way they walked and acted.

The muggers were looking for an easy target and a person who appeared to lack confidence and awareness. In 1992 CBS News in New York did a similar study asking would-be muggers from high crime areas the same question. Not surprisingly the answers were very similar. They found their marks by the way they carried themselves.

Being aware is truly the key, but putting yourself in that sort of heightened awareness twenty-four hours a day is an unrealistic expectation. Once in a while we find ourselves using poor judgment or placing ourselves in risky situations. Being upset with yourself when this happens solves nothing and can even create a greater risk as you lose focus. Making mistakes is okay. We all make mistakes. How you turn it around and learn from it is the key.

Let me give you an example from my own life.

Once I was driving alone in a strange area and got lost. It happens. I pulled up to what I thought was a restaurant and opened the passenger window of the car to ask for directions. There were two men walking down the sidewalk at the time and as I leaned over all smiles one of them pushed right into my window. Well of course I realized I had done everything I tell my students not to do, but it didn't matter once the mistake was made. The only thing that mattered was finding a way out.

I glanced down and realized I was still in drive. My thought was gun the gas and drive and not care what happened to this hoodlum trying to frighten me. I made that my reality, and it must have shown on my face because the man jumped back and said "Lady, I was only joking with you."

Just like that, the situation was defused. All because

I didn't make myself a target – even after making a huge mistake.

In self-defense situations, there are several things that you need to be aware of. Knowledge is power the same as physical strength is power, just in a different way.

Knowledge of the law is important in self-defense situations. Just because you can kick someone into oblivion doesn't mean that you should. Your actions should be appropriate to the situation. For example, if someone touches your shoulder in a menacing way and you respond with a blow that leaves a bruise or breaks a bone, you have responded with excessive force. Police officers won't want to hear that you were trained to act like that. Anyone familiar with the martial arts knows that those who train in dojos with a proper sensei are trained to use restraint and common sense. While it is important to act when you know a physical defense is necessary it is equally important to not become the thing you are defending against. You can't become the villain, the bully, the thug. You have to be better than that.

Know your assets and your weaknesses, and stay within your own abilities. Use your strengths, whether it is running, kicking, punching, or even talking. If you can talk your way out of trouble without ever throwing a punch, you've won the fight before it even begins. When necessary, use the weapons of your body.

If defense is necessary and you take action...do

anything you need to in order to escape with your life. This includes looking around you and utilizing things like the contents of your purse or pocket as well as environmental resources for defense purposes.

In researching information for a paper I presented at Long Island University the statistics I found showed that the farther removed in relationship a person is from you the more likely you are to talk your way out of the situation (my sources included "Criminal Victimization in the United States" 1992 page 69, the National Crime Victimization Survey based upon 400,000 interviews from 1987 – 1991, amongst others). The better you are acquainted with the person the less likely you are to talk your way out of that situation.

I tend to feel that the same applies to the physical defense. The less you know the individual the more likely you are to take action when you feel it is warranted while the more acquainted you are with the person you begin to doubt whether or not they mean to harm you causing you to wait too long to take proper action. These same statistics support this when stating that the 42.8 % of the attacks against women reportedly occurred in or near their home or that of a friend. To me it signals the fact that these are areas where we feel more secure and tend to lower our guard.

Another statistic that I found interesting and one that backed up my concept that we are the one in charge of our own safety showed that in over 60% of the time self-defense measures taken by the victim worked while someone intervening on your behalf helped in less than 40% of the cases. One reason I believe this to be so is because a person mugging you who suddenly find themselves up against a good Samaritan or other assistant will have to do away with you quickly creating even greater damage than originally anticipated. The other statistic backing up my theory is that taking self defense measures hurt your situation in less than 10% of the time and in another 10% of the time did no harm at all. It makes sense then for you to -- take responsibility for your own safety -- harness fear energy and use it to your own advantage. According to the Bureau of Justice Statistics -- Criminal Victimization in the United States- 1992, "The violent crimes of rape, robbery and assault -- which involve a threat or an act of violence in confrontations between victims and offenders -- are considered the most serious crimes measured by the NCVS1 , twenty percent of all crimes measured by the survey were violent crimes." Out of 140,930 reported rapes in 1992 - 40,730 were completed while 100,200 were "Attempted." How many were not reported?

The statistics researched prove that self-defense of any nature works in up to 71% of violent attacks while it hurt in only 9%. 8% of the time it could have gone either way and in yet another 12% of the time it neither helped nor hurt. Viewed in this manner it is obvious that in about 83% of the time it is worth doing something. Anything is better than standing by and becoming a victim. The program helps people get in touch with themselves and learn what it takes to avoid victimization.

Finally, listen to your instincts. If something doesn't feel right then it probably isn't. We were given a gift of perception that we all too often ignore. For some, this "sixth sense" is more highly attuned then it is in others. This is something you must develop from within. Being a victim can mean a lot of things to a lot of people, good or bad, but the most important thing is how we feel about ourselves on the inside. Hindsight is a wonderful thing but it is only there after the fact. "Should haves," "would haves," and "could haves" are not empowering emotions. If you want to be in charge of your life you need to make the decision to take control of your life – TODAY.

We learn from our experiences and move on, otherwise we become victims over and over and over.

BE A VICTOR NEVER A VICTIM

Marilyn Fierro

Chapter 8 – New Challenges

When we initially opened the Smithtown Dojo in 1978 we had the entire upstairs to use, although it was broken into smaller rooms. The rent increased over the years and eventually the landlord decided to split the upstairs and create an apartment in the rear of the building. The remaining space was not going to work for us so the students banded together and offered to break down some walls, enlarging the dojo by combining my office room with the current workout section. Some of the students even rode the Long Island Railroad to town with tools to help out. It was an amazing time and I was fortunate and grateful to have an electrician and carpenter amongst my students at that time.

Our story was even picked up by the local news. It was quite the human interest piece, our little group making due with what we had to follow our passion. The renovated dojo worked well for many years. We were so successful, in fact, that the landlord decided to double my rent. No negotiations worked and there was no way for me to be able to pay what he was asking. I started looking for other places but the rent was always way out of my range. Then again, so was the rent where we were.

I was still teaching at the Suffolk Youth Jewish Community Center and the program was doing well so I began making plans to move the dojo to that location. After several meetings I realized that once there I would have to become SYJCC staff and go to all their meetings and perform other duties. That was not going to work for me.

I returned to the dojo that day quite disheartened with no idea about what I was going to do next. I walked around getting more depressed and wondering if I was going to fix this. Then I began wondering why I was even bothering. It was a spiral that took me further and further down until I recognized what I was doing to myself. I had set myself up to fail over the last year with all this negative thinking.

It was just like the training I used in my dojo. Once I recognized the mistake I had made to put myself in a bad situation, I could use what I had at hand to get myself out. Instead of doubting my place as a wife, a mother, a martial artist and especially a sensei, I used my belief in my purpose. I told myself to take one last walk through town to see if there were any affordable locations I had missed in my funk. Because I chose to meet the problem head on, I found success.

It might not have been what I wanted but there was a basement room available. There were two bathrooms in the hallway and a room big enough for a parent lounge. Again the students chipped in and set to clearing the place, building closets, making a section for my office and locker rooms. My husband and my boys helped as well.

Doug Prato was athletic director at one of the local High Schools and he got us old wrestling mats for the floor. Mirrors were moved from the first dojo and the students loaded trucks or walked down the street with equipment. We had a new home at 135 West Main Street. Within a year we were able to expand to an upper level office and again remodeled the downstairs dojo, adding windows for the parents to continue viewing classes. We were there for a total of twenty-five years...before that landlord sold the building.

The new landlord decided to repair the building from the top down and managed to flood the lower level on several occasions. Then the oil burner went in the heart of winter causing me to close the dojo numerous times. So much went wrong and it was time to leave. My confidence in the place had run out. Thirty-seven years with a dojo is a pretty good run.

The writing had been on the wall for a while but I did not want to tell the students I needed to close until I could find a new place. There were several options available to take space in other places but none of them felt right to me, whether it was the rent or the hours available or something else.

Presently, thanks to my student Ken Moncayo, I have a new home two days a week at Smithtown United Methodist Church. We make it as much like a dojo as we can, and the best part is that I am free to travel on the weekends to tournaments or teach seminars. I'm finally where I'm meant to be.

At my moment of doubt with that first dojo there was a spark of inspiration, a realization that my own faulty thoughts may have brought me to the brink of losing what I loved so much. Yet, once I made myself do what I knew was best, that's when the epiphany came and helped me to create a new and better dream.

Chapter 9 – My Spiritual Connection

For the uninitiated, it may be hard to fathom the spiritual component that exists within the martial arts culture. Martial arts is more than just a form of self-defense, or a good workout, or anything of the sort. It is a way of life. A total way of life that requires dedication and devotion.

By 1982, my spiritual connection to the martial arts had began to blossom as my skills in karate grew. I was a Nidan (second rank Dan) and running my own dojo as well as teaching at the Suffolk YJCC. My training led me into the deeper mysteries of a body's energy and I began to work with crystals and stones to produce various types of energy. I was able to show how ki (you may be more familiar with it pronounced as "chi") worked through the use of crystals. Ki is that internal energy we can all tap into if we know how. The very energy of life. I practiced sending my energy out to the crystal to make it move and withdrawing my energy to stop it again. This concept is much the same as a ninja's invisibility. It is one thing to camouflage oneself but another not to have one's presence felt. Our energy can be strong enough to repel someone or it can draw a person in. In the case of a ninja the person's energy is withdrawn to the point that their presence is not felt.

These practices helped me focus. It helped me become a better person to know there is an internal reserve that I could tap into and use to help myself, my family, and the people I encountered every day.

Sharing your concepts of energy and the spiritual realm is not something many are open to, but finding someone who feels the same way you do, or is at least willing to listen to your ideas, can be like finding a new friend. Part of the martial arts culture, part of our energy if you will, comes from spreading information about what we have learned. Not to those who won't listen. Just to those who are willing to sit, and talk, and hear us.

I encourage you to observe some of the synchronicities (perceived as coincidences) throughout this book. Then, at the end, we can reconnect for a broader discussion of my journey into the energetics of life and the martial arts.

Chapter 10 – Shows, Features, and Awards

Things have a way of leading into one another and creating a flow to our lives. I used to go out to Gurney's in Montauk once a year with my best friend Kathy Natalie. There was a psychic named Lois there that we would go to. One day she asked me what I did because my cards were always interesting to her. When I told her I taught martial arts she was so excited that she invited me back to be on her show "The Lois Wright Show" on LTV, their local cable station.

I had a team of kids, including my son Steven, go out to the Hamptons to film the show. I started the show showing off some warmup exercises. After introducing me, Lois asked who I had brought.

In preparation for the show I had the kids ready to

start with sit-ups. When Louis asked me their names I could not see their faces with their knees up so I asked them to sit up and introduce themselves.

We went on with the show and everything seemed fine until the people in the production booth realized they couldn't get a shot of Lois and me with the table between us. So, off camera they came behind me and picked up my chair *with me in it* and moved it closer to Lois, dropping me and the chair down.

The chair slammed down on my foot and broke my little toe.

I managed to catch my breath and continue with the interview and demonstration. My son was sitting up in the production booth and later told me that when we were running out of time Lois was so into the show that the producer was jumping up and down trying to get her attention that it was time to end. I felt her energy, and I felt mine, and it allowed me to continue even through my pain. Could I have stopped? Certainly. Should I have stopped? Well, that's a matter of opinion. In my opinion, my ki would not have let me stop.

Two things happened after that day. First, when I received my copy of the show I brought it to our local cable station and managed to have it aired in my area as well. The second was that our show was a finalist in the Long Island Film Festival as an educational film.

In the 1980s I was developing an Attack Prevention Program, which I began to teach in Long Island High Schools. I wanted to teach the physical education teachers so they could continue the training after I had moved on. I needed an instructional tape for the program and there just wasn't any out there that met my message. I'd have to do it myself.

So, I asked around. The first people I approached wanted to charge up to $10,000 to make this video for me. Thankfully the school system had a BOCES program. The Board of Continuing Educational Services for New York State (BOCES), is a vocational school where students learn a trade by doing hands-on work. So, I was lucky enough to get the BOCES audio visual program to make the video for me.

It took sixteen weeks of filming and about the same amount of time for editing on top of it. As it turned out, this was during one of the snowiest winters and school was cancelled many times. I had the footage and no one to edit! So once again, I learned a new skill. I began to learn how to splice sequences together and keep a record of times and sections. In the end it was a great learning experience and a sixty minute "Attack Prevention" tape was created.

Fierro Sensei demonstrating self-defense with unorthodox tools.

It became part of my program. Eventually, that tape and program went into eleven Long Island High Schools. I am truly amazed that I have had that sort of impact on people, through my dedication and my drive, and my love of martial arts.

Since I had videos and training programs, I was once invited to appear with Dave Porello in five different five-minute clips that aired on the Home Shopping Network. Dave's show consisted of a lot of talking and I wanted action. There's not much that can be packed into five minutes so I got frustrated. I gave them the abbreviated version of self-defense. I had stuffed a bunch of smaller weapons in my Gi and laid out things from my purse around me, and I just started going one to the other on my poor unsuspecting student who was there to help me demonstrate. No one got hurt, mind you, and in retrospect it was quite funny.

Eventually I was invited to appear on a TV show hosted by Councilwoman Pam Green called *Women in the 90s*. It was a fifteen minute show and since I had no one to help me I used a portion of one of my tapes as my introduction. That show led to a full page color story in Newsday's Smithtown section about my program. From there Cablevision's Channel 12 news picked up the story and asked to film a class. I set one up at my dojo and they filmed a session. It seemed like hours of filming and interviews from participants. The following day I went to the studio to introduce the course and then the footage was aired. What took hours boiled down to ten minutes and a quick introduction by me. The editing was good and the sound bites captured what needed to be conveyed.

One small success leads to others, but you first have to believe and cultivate an energy of success. Then...take action.

Over the years many wonderful awards have been presented to me, and while some stand out more than others, all have a special place in my life. I believe if you stay on track doing what you are meant to do, recognition will come.

The first award to take my breath away was being inducted as the second woman and first martial artist into the Jewish Sports Hall of Fame. I had no idea the magnitude of this event. They show a video of the accomplishments of each inductee. Inductees were obviously Jewish individuals but each one had made an impact on others and helped in one way or another outside of the individual art. I was inducted with such notables as Red Sarachek, Harry Danning, Bill Mazer and Barny Ross. After the induction ceremony there was a panel discussion led by the MC, Barry Landers. All of these men were far older than myself and most of the audience who stayed were senior citizens. As I began to listen to their stories it was not about their accomplishments as athletes or coaches but as people who cared enough to help others be better in any way they could. By the second speaker I raised my hand and asked if I too could say something. I told everyone I that I did not feel worthy of being on the panel but after hearing what they had to say it was all exactly how I too felt.

Jackie Robinson once said, "A life is not important except for the impact it has on others." I too believe that.

Later that day I was signing many programs and even a baseball bat, but it was the short interview by the reporter from WALK FM that stood out to me the most. The reporter asked simply, "What will you do next?"

I had just been promoted to 7th Dan, making me the

highest woman recognized in almost all Isshinryu associations worldwide and now received this awesome honor inducted into a permanent hall of fame. It really let me know that I was doing something to touch people's lives and to motivate them so they can be the best they can be. Really, what could be better than this? I honestly had no answer.

I hesitated so long his next question was, "What do you love?" I thought, "Besides family and karate... what else is there?" I suddenly realized it was TV work that had inspired me the most. After all, I had made one tape and had been on TV several times already. So I told him I would like to have a TV show on martial arts but also on anything that will make people better. His answer was, "Then do it."

That spring of 1997 I went to Cablevision and inquired about getting a show. I was told that I would need to take an educational course and acquire a crew of at least seven people. I had no idea where I would get seven people available at the same time but I would try. I think I ended up with about five.

We took the course on how to use the equipment as well as using the studio to film. I told the manager that we would most likely be filming away from the studio after the course was complete, which was fine by him. Now all I needed was a title for my show.

I went to the Heilman's Annual Training Camp in Pennsylvania and there was a man named Angel Lemus who had a publication. I had my attack

Prevention Tape with me and we spoke a lot about it. He agreed to print my story, "Victor or Victim," in the next issue. We spoke about the TV show and I guess I kept repeating that I wanted people to be able to take charge of their lives. He said, "Then just call your show *Taking Charge*." That settled the matter.

To date I have over 130 shows covering different forms of martial arts as well as a variety of healing modalities, spiritual channeling, guide dogs, therapeutic horses, and, yes, crystals. Catherine Boll was one of my first volunteers and was already into film and video so she offered to help with some location shots. I was able to sign out an SVHS Camera from the studio and began to shoot whatever and wherever I could. Scott Danziger ,who lived in the area, also offered to assist. Over the years Scott has been not only a great help as my videographer but he also included many clips from my Taking Charge shows on the Uechi Ryu web page which he had been webmaster.

Around 1997 Joel Chandler and Tim McGhee came to Long Island for our Isshinryu Friendship Tournament with Grandmaster Uezu Angi. It was a truly great event with Don Nagle and Don Bohan attending as well. Nick Adler Sensei was approached by Chandler and McGhee Senseis, who asked for support in nominating me for the Isshinryu Hall of

Fame. They specifically said they wanted me to be the first woman inducted.

Sensei agreed and officially nominated me, which helped pave the way for my induction in 1998. This was the same year Don Bohan, who had passed away in February, was also inducted. It was truly an honor not only to achieve another first but to be included at the same time as my dear friend.

Marilyn Fierro

Chapter 11 – Influences

As long as I can remember, Nick Adler Sensei has gone to every training seminar he possibly could. He also encouraged students to go, which was not always the case when it came to senior instructors. Many wanted students to remain cloistered in the small world the head sensei built. Certainly, the ability to train with others in a different style even for a short time makes for not just a better martial artist but a better tournament official as well.

Sensei introduced me to so many instructors and systems over the years it is difficult to list everyone... but I would like to talk a little about some.

I have been blessed to know many martial artists from the Isshinryu lineage and most have made an impact on my life in one way or another. I'd like to take a moment and mention a handful of individuals that have impacted my life and training in a positive way.

Rick Adler

Rick Adler (Nick Adler's son), is a great martial artist. I once told him how much he had helped me as I began my training and how much I appreciated it. He said, "Why do you think I helped you?"

I responded, "I think it's because you felt sorry for me."

"No," he said, "it's because seemed like a good person and tried hard to get better."

Rick often competed at tournaments. I remember one occasion where he won first place in kata, kumite, weapons and grand champion in both forms and fighting. His final fight was quite heated and well executed. By the time it was over his mouthpiece had flown across the ring along with the cap from his tooth and his Gi was in shreds. He had beaten Isaac Henry's son who, himself, was a fantastic fighter. Rick was such a good friend to me, especially in the early days of my training and competing.

Don Nagle

Don Nagle was the first pioneer to bring Isshinryu to the United States and a direct student of our founder, Master Shimabuku Tatsuo (1901 - 1975). He was recognized in August 1987 by all the heads of Isshinryu as 10th Dan and leader for Isshinryu.

Harold Mitchum

The next pioneer to bring Isshinryu to the United States was Master Harold Mitchum (1933 - 2016). He was not my teacher but became a good friend through my relationship with his wife, Glenda, and our love of dogs. Glenda and I would share emails and occasional phone calls and I would look forward to our times together. That summer after her passing Master Mitchum brought an album of Glenda's photos for me to see to the Isshinryu Hall of Fame in Tennessee. I was center referee in one of the rings for a long time and he patiently waited for me to finish working so that we could sit, and talk, and share memories of her. It was a memorable time and a very special day for me.

Posing in front of an image of Master Shimabuku Tatsuo. Seen left to right: Harold Mitchum, Marilyn Fierro, John Bartusevics

Harold Long

I believe it was Harold Long who was next to bring Isshinryu to the United States. Adler Sensei was at the very first Hall of Fame and IIKA Tournament, Banquet and Induction Ceremony in 1980. I was at just about every one that followed and for many years Master Long (1930- 1998) would pick us up at the airport even when the event moved from Knoxville to Pigeon Forge.

One time our flights were delayed and a funny thing happened. After sitting on the tarmac and finally returning to the terminal thinking we would be late for the banquet, we found out that the person cooking for that evening's banquet was on the same flight. When we finally landed we realized we did not have a ride to get to the induction ceremony!

Doug was heading to the same place he offered to give us a ride. He and his wife and daughter were all rather large in build and their ride was a Toyota Corolla. Not a car meant to be used as a taxi, that's for sure. The three of them squeezed into the front and Sensei, Kevin Nentwich and I squished ourselves into the back. It was a white-knuckle drive to their house to say the least. I vividly remember Doug's wife saying, "My father told me never to use the brake." She must have taken her father's advice because for the entire ride, she never did.

When we were close to their home she made a right turn on to a road and stayed on the wrong side of the two way street. A car was coming at us from the other way suddenly, and the three of us in the back stared open-mouthed as Doug's wife kept going straight at it. Doug said, calm as could be, "Honey, there's a car coming." She said, "I know but I have to make a left here."

Well as you can tell because I'm writing this for you now, we survived. We made it to the Park Plaza hotel in Pigeon Forge with no other complications. Doug, bless him, sent us a basket of fruit, cheese and crackers as his way of apologizing.

Steve Armstrong

Lastly came Steve Armstrong (1931-2006), I started going to his tournaments in Connecticut and loved spending time with this kind man. It was also the tournament where I always seemed to do well as it would be held in a hotel where some rings were carpeted like my dojo.

On September 9, 1977 after arriving in Texas preparing to present a martial arts ranking system to practitioners of Karate, Sensei Armstrong was in transit to his mother's home planning to stop at his father's cemetery, he suffered an onset of massive head pain and nausea. By the next morning it was obvious he needed to go to the hospital. There they discovered a golf ball-sized tumor in his pituitary gland that had ruptured. After surgery there were further complications that could have taken his life. He told me afterward that his time as a marine and his karate training gave him the will to survive and strength to pull though.

Eventually these health issues caused this once-kind

man to become harsh and difficult. The constant pain got to him, I suppose. When I took some students to his tournament I was shocked to find how he had changed. Eventually it was Lou Lizotte and Steve Young who took over the association. In 1984 Steve Armstrong wrote *Isshinryu Karate* followed by a series of kata books which, to my knowledge, are still available and were far ahead of their time. I remember they included sketches that, when the pages are flipped, will actually animate the different katas. He was always smart about things like that.

Osamu Ozawa

The first multi-style seminar I remember going to was on Long Island with Osamu Ozawa in Shotokan Karate. I believe I was the only woman in a large group of mostly Black Belts. The Isshinryu punch is far different than that in Shotokan and I was definitely struggling with it when Master Ozawa, who was a bit hard of hearing, loudly said "Young Lady" before correcting my punch. I know Adler Sensei must have groaned over that one. Later I showed him my Isshinryu punch and why we did it that way. He was okay with me after that.

I also had the opportunity to train with Kanazawa Sensei in Shotokan, an excellent practitioner and teacher.

Bill Wallace

I learned a lot about kicking from Bill Wallace around 1980 at my first seminar with him and he is still the same great kicker, patient teacher, and person today.

To Marilyn - Best of Luck and best wishes with your club - Bill (Superfoot) Wallace Dec 6, 1980

Dan Inosanto

We traveled to Cortland, NY for Kevin Seaman's camps a few times and trained in Filipino arts with Dan Inosanto, Tai Boxing with Master Chai, and Wing Chun with Francis Fong who has an amazing mastery of ki. I was actually able to follow up my Kali training from Sifu Inosanto with Instructor Neil Cauliffe who had a school in Queens before moving to Florida.

Chuck Merriman

Master Chuck Merriman, who became such a good friend to us over the years, taught seminars at our camps and at Bruce Heilman's IKKF as well. He is an excellent Gojuryu practitioner, competitor, and coach. Master Merriman had Morio Higaonna at his Connecticut Dojo and we trained in the Goju version of Seiuchin. Master Higaonna would walk around checking our Shiko Dache, otherwise known as the sumo stance.

The Heilmans and Odo Seikichi

Adler Sensei was good friends with Bruce and Ann Marie Heilman of Okinawa Kenpo and would go to their camps and training. Through them I was able to film people like Bill Hayes, Miguel Ibarra, and Jody Paul each with their own style and all with a great sense of camaraderie, making for good friends and fun times. Odo Seikichi was the Heilman's Okinawan Sensei. The first time I met Odo Sensei he was teaching tonfa. I had been training and competing with tonfa for quite awhile before then.

Odo Sensei asked me to show him my Hamahiga and he liked it. Then he taught us Odo no Tonfa Ni. Now, I worked Tonfa all the time but never for hours on end. Yes, hours! He taught us and we did the form over and over again, then he told the students to rest. Not black belts though. That was the first time I ever had bloody blistered hands from tonfa.

The Heilmans always had a variety of instructors at their camp, each with their own style, but I loved the times Odo Sensei was able to come. I think I was already a Sandan or Yondan in Isshinryu Karate when I had the chance to test for Shodan in Kobudo with both the Heilmans and Odo Sensei. I cannot even begin to tell you how nervous I was. I had not tested for rank in a very long time. I passed and it went well in spite of my stress. It was such an honor when Bruce and Ann Marie brought Odo Sensei to Long Island and they visited my dojo as well as Sensei's. So much energy in one small man.

Fumio Demura

The first time I met Fumio Demura he was teaching the use of nunchaku. I had never handled one in my life. When we had a break I was standing by myself and he walked over and mentioned my Mizu Gami patch, the water goddess symbol of Isshinryu. A conversation ensued about her symbolism. I could feel a really nice energy from him so I said, "Sensei I am sorry I did not buy your poster, but after speaking with you I would like to do it now."

We went to the desk but there was only one poster left with a little tear in the edge. He said he could not sell that to me but would like to give it to me. He wrote on it in Kanji. I jokingly asked if what he had written meant that I did terrible Nunchaku. He said, "No. It says you have a good heart."

Years later Uezu Sensei was at my dojo and saw that poster on the wall. As he walked by he chuckled. I asked him "Sensei what does it say?" I held my breath just in case but he said, "It says you have a good heart." Phew. I have seen him many times since then and he is beyond wonderful.

Demura Sensei is true Bushido and a warrior in every sense of the word. He followed his dream coming to the Unites States just after WW2 when Japanese were not accepted or wanted. He proved himself time and again as a quality martial artist but also as a kind and considerate man.

I sat next to him several years at the United States Martial Arts Federation banquet. 2016 saw the release of the movie *The Real Miyagi* about his life and his role as the stunt double and subject matter expert for Mr. Miyagi in *The Karate Kid*.

He had been suffering health issues prior to 2015 but has continued to teach and conduct demonstrations. Sue Hawkes of the United States Association of Martial Artists had arranged for a showing of the film and Demura Sensei was there to view it with us. We cheered along with the film at various moving points and at the end he received a standing ovation. He then made his way up the center of the theatre as we stood and continued to applaud. He handed out signed posters to everyone.

It was such an honor to see a movie about his life alongside him. I watched him at the tournament making a little origami bird with such care and precision. Then he reached across and handed it to me. I carefully brought that bird home in a cup so it should not be crushed and it now has a place of honor on my shelf, wrapped in plastic.

Enjoying a moment with Demura Sensei. I'm honored by his friendship.

Sakimukai Masaharu

I had the honor to train with Grandmaster Sakimukai sometime in the late 80s or early 90s. He instructed us in the use of the jo and even though I was not very experienced in that weapon, I loved it. When Sakimukai was teaching it was more of a flow drill, which is something I love doing as it is about energy and feeling the opponent. As I've said, Adler Sensei is very astute and he got the drills faster than I could. He also always looks for a killing blow. Unfortunately there was a point when I was paired off with Sensei and all I was doing was running for my life.

Wally Jay

John Oslager ran seminars called Meet the Masters. Through him I was able to film many fine martial artists for my "Taking Charge" TV shows. One man who was not only a pleasure to work with but was pleased to hear of my show was Professor Wally Jay.

Professor Jay made sure he was at the correct visual angle for the techniques to be visible. His Small Circle Theory was geared well for women and he loved showing me how it worked. Even as we stood together during the interview his hand was already locked and ready for use. He was one of the only people to acknowledge my work, write me a note of thanks, and send me one of his books. He also sent holiday cards from Hawaii. A true gentleman.

Oyata Seiyu

Adler Sensei and Terry Maccarrone were the first to bring Master Oyata to the East Coast. Oyata Sensei was from Kansas and taught tuite and kyusho (pressure point technique) which he used to knock people out. Me, being into energy and its flow through the human body, was very curious about his techniques. After the seminars and tournament we had a dinner. I had a massive headache and decided to leave early. I was saying goodbye to people and of course to Master Oyata. I asked him if he had ever considered using his techniques for other purposes involving a person's energy field and if he could also use his art to heal. He said yes and gave me a big hug. As he did he tapped two fingers on the center of my back and in minutes I felt as if I could have done the entire weekend all over again.

I had the ability to train with him on several other occasions and he always appreciated Isshinryu, especially the way Adler Sensei taught it. He could be really tough but when he worked with me he showed me without pain or damage. If someone challenged him or a move he was quick to take them out and show that he knew his art.

Muang Gyi

Speaking of Spiritual, I first met Doctor Maung Gyi of the Bando System at the Don Bohan / Rick Niemira Memorial event in Virginia. We began speaking and somehow got into a very nice spiritual conversation. After the event Doctor Gyi sent me a copy of his translation of the Burmese Internal Energy System called Min Zin. I found it amazing how in sync it was with what I know through my own training. In the package he included a photo of Adler Sensei and myself with him and a beautiful note to remember to keep up with my meditation classes and let energy fill my life. I cannot say it enough but it is a wonderful feeling to be able to connect with people who share the same values.

Robert Trias

One name that can't be left out of this chapter is Grandmaster Robert Trias of the United States Karate Association, which was the first such association in the States. Adler Sensei had been going to Trias Annual Training before I had the opportunity and always spoke highly of it. I finally had my opportunity in 1984. There were so many great instructors at the training and such a diversity of information. It was a great experience to be part of it. Trias's instructors introduced metaphysical as well as practical training into their seminars.

Joe Lewis

Joe Lewis was an awesome fighter and taught seminars all over the country. I loved watching his techniques but fighting was never my strong point. He and Sensei got along really well as both seemed to have that street mentality. I liked our talks after the training was over where I could see another side of Joe's personality which was more spiritual than his professional persona.

Don Bohan

I met Don "Bo" Bohan and Rick Neimera at the same time in North Carolina. Rick was quite the gentleman and very pleasant, while Bo was crude and not pleasant at all. I did not like him and would avoid him whenever we saw one another. One time I went to get coffee for myself and my Sensei who was speaking with Don, so I offered to get a cup for him as well. When I handed him the cup he said, "Tell me something, you don't like me do you?" I said, "no." So, he asked me why I got him coffee. I told him that I did not like him, but that didn't mean I didn't respect him. This is the way it is in the martial arts.

That night he and I sat up until about three in the morning talking in the hotel lobby and I learned that I had judged this man, who had done three tours of duty in Vietnam, by my own experiences. I learned that night that I was indeed judgmental even though I did not think I had been. Once I put myself in his position I understood why he didn't want to get too close to anyone after living in an environment of never knowing what could happen to a friend at any time. After that day we became fast friends.

After he got on the computer our friendship grew even closer with daily emails. Whenever he knew I had a busy weekend he would send me virtual flowers with a wonderful note. He called me "Sugar", and coming from that tough guy it was quite okay with me. Two of those virtual flowers remain on my wall today. I only wish I had saved them all.

One day we were at a tournament and Bo was wearing a pendant with a silver dragon surrounded by a gold circle and gold chain. I admired it and he took it off and put in around my neck. I was shocked and told him I could not take that. He said he would get another, that it was not valuable and he wanted me to have it. He wouldn't take no for an answer. It is a treasured part of my life and brings him closer each time I wear it.

Over the years Bo would surprise me with many little dragon statues or special objects and discs full of old photos of masters. One time he gave me an angel doll that he and his wife, Joan, had made. Still nothing impacted me as deeply as that one impromptu present from years before.

The last time I saw him was in November of 1997. He was sick at the time but was more concerned about me than himself. He wanted to know if I was going to be okay when he was gone. Can you imagine that? We cried together, both knowing it would probably be our last goodbye.

On February 9, 1998 Don Bohan passed away after losing his battle with cancer. That day I awoke early to a phone call from Leslie Kaiser telling me of his passing. When I walked into my living room a beam of light was coming through the door and lighting up the angel that Bo had made for me. I felt as if he were there. It had never happened before and it has never happen since.

Sometime in 2000 something happened in karate that upset me terribly. I was so distraught I could not relax. We were on the boat and I lay down planning to meditate. Max our Pomeranian got up and went to the back door to be taken to the beach. We had just been there and he had never asked at the boat door before so I figured he really must need to go to the bathroom. I got up and we swam to the beach. He lifted his leg for a second and nothing came out then turned to go back to the boat. Suddenly a Red Rose floated up to me feet. I picked it up and looked at it. My husband called to me and asked if it was a plastic rose it was so perfect. "No," I said, it is a perfect fresh rose.

We went back to the boat and I put the rose into water and went back to meditating. I thought God felt bad for me and sent me a flower, but that did not feel right. Then I said my Mom who had passed in 1994 sent it, and again nothing. I let go of why the Rose had come to me but felt it was a message since Max made me go to the beach. We stopped at a place to eat and began riding home with a beautiful sunset and suddenly I heard the words, "A Rose for You". It was my dear friend Don Bohan who had already passed away. Bo was so spiritual and he once sent me a virtual Rose with dew drops of water on it. I immediately knew it was him. As soon as I returned home I called his wife Joan and she said yes it was him and she remembered the Rose he had sent as well.

The following image is a special keepsake of Bo and I together.

Liu Chang

Michael Calandra once hosted Sifu Liu Chang of Feeding Crane Kung Fu and I was able to attend the seminar. I filmed a *Taking Charge* episode with Sifu Chang and enjoyed watching him "make thunder" with his strikes and mastery of ki. One of the moves he was teaching was a break out of a grab, into double palm heel strikes. I thought that was a great move but never expected him to come to me and say, "You do it." After all, I was the one who was filming. It took me by surprise but I tend to use palm heel strikes for self-defense and am used to sending energy into it as well. So, without thinking I said okay and did the move. It moved Sifu Chang back and the room gasped! Adler Sensei said, "She hit the master!"

I was shocked at myself and felt terrible but Sifu Chang was so funny leaning into me to say, "You are good, but not *that* good." Maybe I can't make thunder like he does, but I *did* make him move.

Mike Stone

Mike Stone was an undefeated martial arts champion and would teach seminars about the mental aspect of fighting. He would talk to the students about having the right mindset and then they would get up and begin kicking and moving with no other warmup. His idea is that he was mentally warmed up and ready to go at a moment's notice. Mike was one of the first people I met who was deeply into meditation. I loved when Sensei and I could spend time with him and his wife Taina.

Nakazato Shugoro

Eberhard Welsch and Dan Smith brought the Okinawan Masters to Washington, DC. Sensei and I went to train with them there. I actually used the opportunity to film a series of show episodes. I first had to ask permission from the patriarch of the group, Grandmaster Nakazato Shugoro of Shorinryu Karate (who later was declared a National Treasure by the Okinawan government). I was told it would be okay to film anyone else but not to film Nakazato Sensei.

There were four seminars going on at the same time and I had a large SVHS Camera which I had signed out from Cablevision. I was walking around with it on my shoulder trying to capture the essence of each instructor. There was a break and I sat down to rest, dripping wet from sweat with the effort of holding the camera up and walking around while everyone else trained.

Nakazato Sensei came over to me and began to talk. He told me he respected women that work hard and appreciated my efforts. He spoke about his wife and what a hard worker she was too. Later he agreed to do an interview with me for the show and had Shimabukuro Zenpo translate as he spoke in Japanese about wanting people to come and train in Okinawa. After the lunch break it was time for him to teach and all the students were lined up to bow in. I sat down to watch when someone came over to me and said, "He wants you to film him..."

What an honor and a special moment. It was 1999,

three months before his 80th birthday. He did sit ups and pushups and then had the group join him. He was amazing!

I was not only able to film but he actually played to the camera and taught some techniques. People told me later that they had never seen him like that. It shows that no matter what stage of life we are at we can still be our very best in whatever we do.

Picture Tour

Fierro Sensei with Joe Lewis in 1985

A happy moment with Peter Urban of Gojuryu fame

Sokeship Hall of Fame with Thomas LaPuppet

Robert Trias – Founder of the United States Karate Association

Guru Dan Inosanto, famed student of Bruce Lee

Renowned fighter and actor Ron Van Clief

Mike Stone seminar. Fierro Sensei kneeling to Stone's left.

With Sue Hawkes and Richard Fields of USAMA

International Karate Kobudo Federation Annual Training in 2014. The event featured notable practitioners such as Jody Paul, Bill Hayes, Ann-Marie Heilman, Bruce Heilman, Nick Adler, Marilyn Fierro, and Miguel Ibarra.

Referee panel featuring Marilyn Fierro, Nick Adler, Ed McGrath,Gary Alexander, Willie Adams, and Don Bohan

Filming with Stacy Sweet of Channel 12 News in 1994

Fierro sensei with Odo Sensei (and matching shirt)

Oyata Sensei in 1984

Nick Adler and Marilyn Fierro with Uezu Angi in 1987

Kichiro Shimabuku, son of Isshinryu founder Shimabuku Tatsuo

Capturing a special moment with Nakazato Shugoro of Shorinryu

Shimabuku Zenpo of Seibukan

Higaonna Morio of Gojuryu

Professor Wally Jay of Small Circle Jujitsu

A special seminar with Professor Muang Gyi of Bando

Jodo training with Sakimukai Sensei in 1985

A chance to train with Oshiro Toshihiro of Shorinryu

Sakimoto Sensei as one of the guest instructors at a special gasshuku

Well known actor and karate practitioner Yamashita Tadashi.

Good friend of many years Demura Sensei after a nunchaku seminar.

Part 2 – Okinawa

Marilyn Fierro

Chapter 11 – First Visit, 1991

My dream since becoming a black belt had been to go to Okinawa, the birthplace of my now beloved Isshinryu Karate. I had trained with Master Uezu on many occasions and he was always inviting me to go there.

All the men I spoke to told me I would not be happy there. They insisted that it was a place where men ruled and women were subservient. I was very nervous that if I ever did get the chance to go, it would be difficult and disappointing.

One day I was in my office, speaking with someone who had asked if I would ever get to Okinawa. I told them of my concerns when suddenly Master Uezu's photo came right out of the frame behind me. It was such incidental timing, such meaningful timing, that it gave me pause. I stopped in mid conversation to pick up the photo. Perhaps, I thought, it was time to reconsider.

As it turned out there was to be a large karate demonstration from all styles on the island and Adler Sensei and I were invited to participate with Master Uezu's group. As soon as arrangements were made for us to come I began to listen to a Japanese language tape and follow along with a booklet that came with it. It wasn't much, but I needed the bare minimum if I was to get by.

We boarded a plane on Wednesday, September 25th excited to be heading on our adventure. By Thursday we landed in Tokyo but unfortunately a typhoon was coming and our flight to Okinawa was cancelled. We were stranded until the next day.

Master Uezu waited for us at the airport even though we landing an hour late and had to wade through security protocols. We were already late for practice for the next day's demo. Off to Camp Foster we went directly from the airport. No time to rest.

It was late and getting later. We practiced Wansu Kata outside as a group. It was so dark I could hardly see, but I guess Master Uezu was satisfied. Finally we were taken to City Plaza Hotel in Okinawa City. It was a very nice place. The room was built like a circle with cubbies and shelves for our belongings. Very different from what one would expect. There was a new robe and slippers for each occupant and pillows filled with beans which I found very comfortable. At first I was disappointed with our surroundings because they were more citified than I had expected in Okinawa. Later, after the demonstrations were complete, our American group – Adler Sensei, Kim Murray, Curt Sawyer and Phil Molinaro – had the opportunity to tour many of the castles and see the countryside. Finally, I would discover the real Okinawa.

The following day was Saturday and the demonstrations were to take place at noon. Master Uezu picked us up early and took us to his house where his wife Yukiko-San made us breakfast. I think it was a bit overwhelming to cook for so many people. Still here we were, in our teacher's home sharing a meal of ham, eggs, toast, and good conversation. We had yogurt milk which no one seemed to like and it was embarrassing as none of us could drink much of it. But we had true Isshinryu spirit and a sharing from the heart.

After breakfast was a visit to the cemetery to pay our respects to Shimabuku Tatsuo, our founder, and ask for his blessing for the demonstrations. The place itself was unimpressive and not in the best repair, but Shimabuku's gravesite had been well tended. I could feel a difference in my own energy the moment I knelt down to meditate and send a prayer to the man I could only wish I had met. Even though I began training in Isshinryu prior to joining Adler Sensei's dojo in 1974 I was not thinking about history or roots. What I was thinking about was how Master Shimabuku had passed away in 1975 and I would never get the chance to meet him.

Finally with the visit over we headed to the huge convention center. Tents had been set up for us to change in and the few women that were there took our turn to don our Gi and get ready. Groups were lined up by schools. Ours was the fourth school to demonstrate and when we were called we ran on to the stage with our hands on our hips lining up as we had practiced. Adler Sensei and I were in the front row along with Kim Murray and Curt Sawyer. Grandmaster Uezu did the introduction and counting. As soon as we had completed our kata we ran off to one side of the stage. Later in the day Master Uezu performed Sunsu Kata and he and Kim Murray did board breaking as well. Everyone seemed to like our performance, but it was not until the next day when the newspapers came out that we found ourselves on the front page of the paper! I was told the translation praised our group of Isshinryu practitioners from America.

The ladies at the front desk of our hotel were so excited, we had become celebrities for the moment.

At that time, I was told, newspapers were only by subscription so the ladies brought in their newspapers and presented them to us. Several of the military personal also helped so everyone could have a copy of the paper.

The travelling Isshin Ryu group conducted a successful demonstration in Okinawa. Uezu Sensei and Adler Sensei are seated front row, center.

The next day, Sunday, we were honored to be able to eat our breakfast at the Camp Butler Officer's Club. What a wonderful American-style meal with fresh omelets and waffles! Then we were off to Ryukyu Mura which was once a working Okinawan farm village and has since become a sightseeing attraction. At that time there was a huge rope that had been used for tug of war between villages and now only comes out for demonstrations. They also had a fight between a Mongoose and a Habu snake. Not something that would be allowed in American culture, to be sure. It seems the Mongoose always wins so they sell wine made from pickling the snake in the alcohol as it ferments, and all kinds of snake concoctions. Sensei bought Okinawan donuts which were so heavy they were impossible to eat, but they sure smelled good!

Later we went higher into the mountains to visit Nakahodo Sensei. He had a small but lovely dojo and a gorgeous home overlooking the ocean. The many pieces of calligraphy and beautifully carved woodwork were all made by him and I admired it as we sat on tatami mats around a low table sharing tea and conversation. When we left we ate dinner at a lovely new hotel nearby with another beautiful view. We all tried Black Black gum. It starts out mint flavored and then gets stronger and stronger with each bite. You should have seen our faces as one by one we got to the really sharp tasting part and then all of us spit out the gum.

That evening Kim Murray tested and passed his Godan exam and soon after a beautiful rainbow appeared in the sky which made me feel as if Master Shimabuku had been watching us that day.

On Monday Master Uezu drove us to Shuri where we stopped and parked on a side road and took photos under the Shuri Gate. Shuri Castle was being repaired so we were only able to explore a small portion of it. We then went to Shureido, a famous martial arts supply store and the owner was a good friend to Uezu Sensei. I ordered black belts for my advanced students with their names on them in Kanji as gifts for covering the dojo while I was away.

Due to renovations the group could only see the Shurei-mon Gate.

Driving in Okinawa in the evenings you can see many fields bathed in light. They are kept on to extend growing time for their produce. Land is at a premium and farming seems to be done anywhere people can find property. The mountain landscapes are dotted with mini cemeteries or mausoleums because there is no other land to put the graves on. Some of them overlook the beautiful Pacific Ocean.

Soon Kim Murray and his group had to leave. We went to his hotel and I asked the lady at the desk in my newly working Nihon-go (Japanese language) how to use the phone. There were pink or green phones and I wanted to call our friend Katherine Loukopoulos to arrange a visit for lunch. She explained which phone to use to call the base and how many yen to put in. The men came down to check out and the desk clerk was trying to tell them something which they did not understand. She pointed at me and said "Ask her she understand." Ha! Apparently, the little Japanese I had learned from my audio tapes wasn't all that bad after all.

Later we went to the laundromat to do a wash. Again, my little booklet came in handy and we waited our turn for the machines. A lady came in and I happened to hear her ask who we were. I guess she wanted to go ahead but I then heard the terms kohai and sempai. These are used to refer to a master and a student in karate, one person who is superior and one person who is subservient in a relationship, but in this case they were talking about washing machine waiting-in-line order! It truly was a different world from the one I knew.

The following day we drove south after going out to breakfast with Master Uezu. We stopped at a pineapple farm and had the sweetest pineapple I have ever tasted. After that it was a visit to Expo which is from the 1975 World's Fair held here in Okinawa.

The grounds and aquarium were very nice but the heat was getting to us. We toured the Aquapolis which is a huge floating structure that had been originally built to evacuate the people of the island should there be a major disaster, or should it sink due to a typhoon. It was designed to detach from its ramps and built to withstand the force of a typhoon and still make it to safety. It has never been needed and remains where it is as an exhibit, floating on the China Sea. We walked to the beach area and I would have loved to dive in and cool off but naturally I never thought to wear a bathing suit under my clothes. Adler Sensei just jumped in with his shorts on. The one time being a man would have been better than being me!

The whole of mainland Okinawa is probably about the size of Long Island in NY and you can easily drive from one end to another in no time at all. That is exactly what we did that day. Master Uezu felt so bad for me not being able to cool off that we drove to Ieki Beach which was two hours away and it was already closed when we arrived. The drive, however, was wonderful. Never have I appreciated air conditioning so much.

We passed Gusikawa City (now called Urumi City) where Master Uezu lives, went by Agena and Kiyan Village, and saw the mountains of Sunsu where they used to collect sea salt. It was an incredible drive that I will always remember.

On the way, we passed two very important islands. Hama Jima, and Higa Jima. My favorite Kata was Hamahiga, named after those two islands. There is a story that surrounds Hama Jima and Higa Jima which Master Uezu told us. The peoples from both islands were arguing over which one was the best. Neither group would give an inch. Both of them insisted their people was the best. Finally they decided to use the rope that we had seen in Ryukyu Mura in a tug of war to decide that decision. Members of each island began to pull the rope and eventually, according to the legend, the island of Higa won, pulling the inhabitants of Hama into the water. In the end they decided to use the name Hamahiga for the Tonfa Kata so no one would fight again.

Wednesday turned into a shopping and packing day

and Thursday we went to pick up our Obi at Shureido only to find they were not ready. Master Uezu decided that he would ship them to me after I got home. We had lunch at a restaurant that had automatic sliding doors. As they opened, they said "Domo arigato gozaimasu. Thank you very much." Even on the expressway when it asks you to take a ticket in Japanese and you wait it will repeat it in English. Chimes sound for messages or to let you know a light has changed. It is all very well organized.

We went to the grocery store and bought bentos (boxed lunches) to bring to the beach. Yes, the beach! Finally I was getting to the beach. And, not just any beach but Chatan Beach on the China Sea. Can you imagine doing Chatan Yara no Sai on the same beach where the great master Yara had practiced?

Finally our whirlwind tour of Okinawa came to an end and we were on our way to Japan.

It was a sad goodbye to Okinawa but I knew this could not be my last visit, there was just so much more to see.

We had some letters of introduction to dojos in

Japan but somehow it just did not work out so we enjoyed some sightseeing instead. Tokyo is a lot like New York but there is an area named Asakusa that has kept the look of old Japan.

We took a day trip to Nikko riding past the Red Sacred Bridge that the Shogun used to come into the area then up the mountain's forty-eight hairpin turns (twenty up and twenty-eight down) looking for the famous Nikko monkeys – snow monkeys who come to bathe in the hot springs of the park. Here above the entrance of the Tosho-go shrine are the Three Wise Monkeys: "See no Evil, Hear no Evil and Speak no Evil."

Further up is Kegon Falls. It had been raining as we went but the rain stopped and was replaced by a cover of fog. I had come all this way to see the falls yet now I could barely see my hand in front of my face. I stood at the edge and said a little prayer that if it was meant to be could the sky clear up for just a minute. Suddenly it was as if God was listening and blew away the fog just long enough for me to capture a quick photo.

We saw Rinno-ji temple and stopped at Lake Chuzenji. Our tour took us to Kamakura and the Great Buddah, the forty-four foot tall bronze statue which sits on the grounds of the Kotokuin Temple, again with pouring rain but the good thing was that

I was able to capture another wonderful photo of the Buddah which surprisingly came out even with the rain. We had many wonderful sites and Temples to visit. My favorite place was Kyoto which had been the original capital of Japan. It is a mixture of old Japanese culture and newer Western culture. Such an amazing place.

A brief moment where the fog cleared and revealed Kegon Falls.

At one point we left the tour to wander around the streets and came upon a gorgeous Budokan. We wandered in and began to watch the women practicing Naginata. After a while their Sensei stepped out on to the floor. The dojo went totally quiet and respectful as they all sat gathered around this older woman with gray sweats on who was giving them a lecture.

After she left they went back to practicing and then took a break. One woman sat near us and I said "joto," meaning good. She laughed and showed me how difficult it was to keep the blade in the correct position after a cut. It was a pleasant exchange. As we toured further we discovered the archery section. Here was a great example of discipline, respect and adherence to tradition. The student would bow, enter and approach the shooting area. After another bow she would lift the bow and carefully place the arrow, take aim, and release. Then with respect, she bowed and left the area. When I looked down the alley to the target the arrow may have missed or hit, it did not seem to matter. What mattered most seemed to be the technique and attitude with which the arrow was released.

At one point our tour was joined by a group of Japanese school girls with their English Sensei hoping to practice English. We had a lot of fun practicing together.

There are so many beautiful areas and wonderful temples to see I hope you, my reader, will one day get to Okinawa and Japan to experience the culture and beauty for yourselves.

Chapter 12 – Return to Okinawa, 1995

In 1995 the Okinawan Prefecture sponsored a tour in the United States with the New York portion hosted by Joe Carbonara, Terry Maccarrone, Nick Adler and Grant Campbell. Several Masters introduced their styles and performed demonstrations. Master Adler was the only American to demonstrate along with them. He received many compliments on his use of the Bo and was presented with a book written by Nakamoto Sensei. The group was there in advance of the Pre-World Tournament that occurred on August 24th to the 28th. Everyone was invited to come to Okinawa and participate.

Here was an opportunity to once again return to Okinawa. We contacted Uezu Sensei and he offered us the opportunity to stay at the dojo which had been built above his house several years before.

Master Uezu met us at the airport with Uechi
Sensei, his wife and daughter, Greg Gudson who
was a new Shodan and secretary to Master Uezu,
and Yagi Sensei. Such a welcome feeling. Then right
from the airport we went to Shuri Castle and had
Soba for lunch before we toured the newly
renovated Castle with it's beautiful view and
gardens. We went to the dojo to bring up our bags
and offer presents to Master Uezu and his wife.
Since this was August when all souls return to their
homeland according to Japanese tradition, it was
Oban Festival time. Still with no rest we went to the
festival along with 150,00 other people celebrating
in various sections. We watched Eisa dancers and
Taiko drummers in the old style while in other areas
the younger generation celebrated with laser lights
and more modern demonstrations of joy.

We were hungry, so Master Uezu went to find us
something to eat. We were talking about it when
some of the Okinawan women heard us and tried to
speak to us in a combination of English and
Japanese. As it turned out they had family in the
U.S. and they offered us food to eat. It was nice to
see people from two separate parts of the world
trying so hard to understand each other. We
thanked them but said we would wait.

When the festivities ended we left, feeling that we
had truly been immersed in the culture and could
bring home a new understanding with us. At the
dojo Master Uezu showed us his photo albums of

the many people he had taught or visited with when they came to Okinawa.

Then he brought out another book and said, "This is your album." He actually had one album of pictures just for our Smithtown Karate Academy. It took my breath away to know he cared that much. I took a photo of him with the album to show my students when we returned. This man from halfway around the world was showing us a deep respect and admiration that we returned tenfold.

Uezu Sensei presenting a special album to Smithtown Karate Academy

We had arrived several days before the tournament so Master Uezu took us to see Master Shimabuku's grave to pay our respects which, to me, is always a spiritual experience. We visited several castles and the dojo program at Camp Courtney. We also visited the Uezu Family Cemetery where he showed us that his family follows similar, but not identical, practices to the Okinawan.

We went to Agena to meet with Shimabuku Shinsho (Ciso), the second son of Shimabuku Tatsuo. Soke Shimabuku's surviving wife, Uto, was living there at the age of eighty-six. Believe it or not, this is the average age for Japanese women. It is a respectable, venerable age but the home did not reflect the honor this woman had earned through her life. It was sad to see the state of the house. Not long after this she would be moved to an assisted living home, where she would continue her long life, well into her nineties.

Visiting the ancestral plot of the Uezu family. The tomb was of rough-edged, ancient stone.

Master Uezu had bought Adler Sensei and myself airplane tickets to Kume Island where he wanted to show us the Uezu family's ancestral home. His family was from Saipan and his father held the title of Pechin which is similar to the rank of Samurai. The house itself was constructed in 1754 and is absolutely beautiful, with well-tended gardens all around. It's as though it has been preserved in time. There was a well in front and while we were there Master Uezu started doing Wansu Kata pointing out the dumping move chanting, "Pick him up and throw in well he can't get out!" It was plain to see the joy this man had at being home again.

Uezu Angi Sensei at his ancestral home.

Sharing a laugh in front of a well, reminded of Uezu Sensei's story of Wansu kata.

If September in Okinawa was hot, August was even hotter. The dojo had one room to wash in and another to dry in. By the time I would wash and wrap something around to get to the next room I was already drenched in sweat again. I would come out and try to do my hair by the dojo mirror but that was always unsuccessful. If a towel was wet it seemed to stay that way even in the sun, because the humidity never let it dry.

When we trained in the evenings we could open the windows up but by night time when we were ready to sleep the rains would come and we had to close the windows to keep the water off the wooden floors. Master Uezu had bought us giant floor fans to stay cool – or rather, less hot – and cots to sleep on.

Usually when someone stayed at the dojo they slept on the floor on quilts out of respect. Bless him for thinking of giving us cots instead, but the mattresses were only about one inch thick and I could not sleep. Every night I would pile more and more quilts on the bed and finally there came a night that we did not have to get up early so I piled even more quilts and finally, on that night, I slept through. I guess I'm not ready to immerse myself totally in the Okinawan traditions...

I had just emerged that next day from the dressing room when I heard Uezu Sensei's footsteps on the stairs. I had been making the bed early so he would not see how I was fixing it up for my American body. He walked into the room and saw my bed piled with all the quilts before I could react. I felt absolutely mortified! He looked at me, and I thought, here it comes the lecture on how I must be better able to withstand a little discomfort. Instead, all he said was, "Oh, Marilyn-san...bed you no like?"

One night I had gone to the bathroom using my flashlight and above the toilet was a giant green bug with red eyes. Being a person who normally puts bugs outside rather than squash them, I scooped it into a towel and held the ends tight. The darn thing started bouncing around in the towel so I started screaming, "Open the door, open the door!"

I still laugh when I think of how this scene must have looked. Me, the creator of several self-defense training videos and one of the most confident people I know, screaming like a maniac because a bug was jumping in a towel!

Another night I kept waking up to someone knocking at the door but no one was there. This seemed to happen every half hour. I finally woke Adler Sensei up to check on it but he had the same lack of success. I was thinking of all sorts of answers that included ancestral ghosts and stray energy from our shared experiences, to local kids playing a prank. As it turned out, there was a gekko behind a picture on the wall...and it was mating season. The little critter was just calling for a mate but each time he extended his throat the picture would bump on the wall creating the knocking sound.

During the week our travel group had practiced Sunsu Kata for our demonstration at the convention center but I do not think it came together as a group until just before our time to go out. Each time we had practiced we were missing a few members or had to incorporate unexpected guests. In the end it all went well. It was the climax of our trip, and we represented our dojo with great energy and dignity.

I had been writing for various martial arts publications for years at this point and this time I was to write an article on this event for Black Belt Magazine. The fact that I was a writer gave me many opportunities to speak with officials and move around more freely.

Japanese school girls carried signs for each team of international competitors for the opening procession into the Convention Center. Later they also directed competitors to the correct rings for their divisions. There were also seminars from top martial artists and we were given a certificate which was stamped by the seminar instructor when we attended their session. It was a great experience, and would have made for a fantastic article.

Unfortunately, there was one single accident to mar the day. In one of the black belt fighting divisions a South African team member was hit with a roundhouse kick to the back of his head and was brought to the hospital. I found out later that he had died two days after that. There had been several other injuries, of course (after all, this was martial arts competition), but none of the other injuries were as severe as that.

It was sad that what had started out as a gesture of peace and goodwill became clouded by this terrible tragedy. When I finally submitted my comprehensive article to Black Belt Magazine the only part they included was one paragraph about the death at the event. They skipped over all the positive aspects of our experience and chose to focus on this instead. It is a reality of life that tragedy makes for good copy, but I cannot tell you how disappointed I was that this should be what people remembered from this amazing experience.

On this visit we were able to connect with Kathy Loukopoulos, a well-known competitor and organizer on the island. We had lunch together and Adler Sensei and I went to teach at her program on Camp Foster. We received a lovely certificate from the Military which I still cherish.

When the Pre-World tournament and seminars came to an end the group from Argentina had no place else to stay and wanted to come to the dojo with us. No way was I going to stay there with that many people so Sensei and I checked into a hotel.

Hurray for air conditioning! I started to feel human once again. Not that I would ever tell Master Uezu that, of course. I was still embarrassed by him catching me with all those blankets on my cot.

Uezu Sensei drove a group of us to Nago and then to Moon Beach. Cantore from Argentina was in the back of the car with me and kept wanting to speak Spanish, whereas I wanted to continue practicing my Japanese. He wanted me to ask Master Uezu to promote him to Nanadan (7th Dan), explaining he had been with Uezu for 5 years. He was 4th Dan and I was 6th dan at the time. When I told Master Uezu what he wanted he said he would not promote him higher than 5th Dan. Uezu Sensei is kind and generous, but he is not to be taken advantage of.

I had always wanted to get a photo by a waterfall like I would see many martial artists pose. Master Uezu brought us to one that he knew after hearing me say what I wanted. It turned out to be a low tide and many of the rocks were exposed without much water flow, but I wanted to be like the guys and go to the top. Well, despite my determination, the men were stronger and managed to get to the top okay but I was struggling on the slippery rocks. Not giving up, I approached a group of children who were diving off the rocks and asked for their help. Between my limited Japanese vocabulary and their limited understanding of English and a lot of sign language, I managed to ask them to help me.

Rather than be embarrassed by what I had done, I feel this is another way of expressing my determination. Never be afraid to ask for help when you need it, or recognize your own physical limitations. Always work hard to overcome them. Always tell yourself you can even when others tell you that you can't. Find a way. Reach the top.

Okinawa is so very different from what I know. For a car wash you drive up and it is the building that moves over the car. Land is at a premium so that works just fine. The radiator went on Master Uezu's van so he brought it to the service station and they could not fix it that day and there were no loaner cars so the owner gave us his new Mercedes to use until the van was repaired. They actually delivered the van to his house when it was done. When you pull into a service station for fuel it is like the old Texaco stations of the 40's or 50's where someone comes to pump gas and another person comes out to check the oil and clean the windshield. A different world in time, in mannerisms, and in thinking.

We spent more time in Okinawa on this visit than our first one back in 1991. We saw so much, experienced the people and the culture, really lived in the place that is so dear to my heart. To watch the smile on the face of my Okinawan Sensei as he would show us something of his world, and to share this experience with Adler Sensei, left me with a deep sense of completion. What could possibly be better?

Chapter 13 - Okinawa, Mo Ichi Do, 2007

Through the years Master Uezu would come to the United States to teach his many students across the country, but over the past several years he has been unable to return due to his health. When too many years had seemed to pass not only for my return to Okinawa and to see Master Uezu I formed a trip with Rita Mensch, the second person I ever promoted to the rank of Black Belt, and headed across the globe once again. It had been eleven years since I'd last been to Okinawa, and I was definitely looking forward to going back.

We left on New Year's day and arrived on January 2nd in Okinawa after a long twenty-three hours of travel. We were greeted at the airport by a smiling Master Uezu who was obviously so pleased we had come. His 73rd birthday was the following day and it was our plans to spend that day with him.

We awoke the next morning excited to start this new Journey in Okinawa. For Rita it was her first visit and initially she could barely speak a word of Japanese but in no time she had people complimenting her on how well she spoke the language.

Uezu Sensei brought us home to see his wife. Recovering from a recent stroke she was unable to join on our journey. We had a good time with her and she remembered me from her previous visit to our dojo in the U.S. We spoke about children and I showed her my grandson's photos and Rita shared pictures of her girls. It was a very pleasant visit for all of us.

Uezu Sensei had also suffered two strokes in the recent past, but he is stronger than most and something of a miracle compared to others in his situation. His doctors attribute his rapid improvement to his martial arts training. I tend to agree. Sensei never gave up, he trained all the time, in both body and mind.

Today, his medical condition has slowed him down of course, and he finds it difficult to communicate, especially in English, but he is still a giant in the world of martial arts and his wisdom is still valued and sought out. He is indeed an inspiration to anyone who has had to overcome a disability.

After a visit to his home we then went to visit the gravesite of the founder of Isshinryu Karate-do. In

Okinawa monuments are erected along the mountainside where the cremated remains of many family members have come to rest. Soke Shimabuku's wife, Uto, had passed that summer so it was especially important to pay our respects to both of them. We felt so honored when Master Uezu knelt down and introduced us to Shimabuku Sensei. He asked him to watch out for me and the Smithtown Karate Academy students and to help us. I believe this was indeed the start of what was to be as much a spiritual journey as it was a quest for knowledge, training and understanding the culture of the Okinawan People.

A fond memory of spending time with Shimabuku Uto, wife of Tatsuo.

We spent the rest of this day touring a variety of places on Okinawa. Some things had changed in the eleven years that I was away but the spirit and kindness of the Okinawan people remained the same. Whenever Sensei introduced me people would become so excited. He would say, "This is Marilyn-san, Hachidan (8th degree black belt)," and a whole conversation would follow from that simple starting point. I looked at Sensei to see what they were saying and he would tell me that in all of Okinawa the highest woman was only 7th Dan. What an honor to be introduced by my Okinawan Sensei at such a high rank.

Karate is obviously a great part of the Okinawan culture. People who train in karate are considered first for employment and highly respected. It is understood that a black belt in karate means a person has an understanding of good work ethics, dedication, and perseverance. Certainly, it would be a prize to have someone like that in your employ. Karate is so important to the culture that some famous living martial artists (usually over eighty years of age) have been declared national treasures for the Okinawan people.

No visit to Okinawa is complete without a stop at Shuri Castle and Shuri Gate. The next day we journeyed to Naha (home of Gojuryu Karate) and had a visit to Shureido Martial Arts Store, a must-do on any martial artist's agenda. Mister Nakasone was happy to see us and is always happy when Master Uezu arrives.

When Master Uezu opened his dojo in 1992 Shureido donated two large mirrors to him. We took photos outside this famous location before moving on to Shuri Castle. For Rita it was wonderful to see these sites for the first time but for me, with my previous experiences here, I was saddened to see that progress had modernized the parking and entryways and taken something away from their historical appearances. I liked our visits in `91 and `95 when we would just drive past the gate, park on the road and walk into the castle.

During our stay we traveled backroads to visit a waterfall, sugar cane fields, a pineapple farm and other sites we would not have seen on our own without Uezu Sensei being with us. There is a tour there that took people around the pineapple field. I had a moment of panic as Uezu Sensei turned to me and said, "You drive." They drive on the left side of the road in Okinawa, and how was I supposed to adjust to that? He began laughing at my expression and explained to me he was only joking. It was an automated ride.

What made it even more special was when he took my hand and turned to me to ask, "Marilyn-san, are you happy?" He wanted this visit to be special and memorable and did everything he could to see that we had a good time. It was everything I could have hoped for and more, a trip never to be forgotten. Wherever we went he would meet people and either know them or make them new friends by the time we moved on. He was so proud of me as a karate teacher and told everyone we met all about me. He is that kind of man, special in every way. I cannot imagine anyone not liking him.

Master Uezu took us to Hamaya beach which is an area with a particularly beautiful view of the Pacific Ocean. He had told us the night before to be ready early that day and to wear our Gi's, because we were going to take pictures. This might have been the one time that his knowledge of his home country failed him because when we got to the area he had chosen, the steps leading down this steep hill in a wooded area were broken, the railing cracked and falling down as well. Only the week before it was fine when he had been down to the beach.

We were so disappointed but Master Uezu didn't let it dampen his spirits. He insisted that we should go down and take many photos for him. We did as we were told including a short video of kata, which didn't work well as sand got kicked up into the camera. This day turned out to be our first cold and windy day, but the view was so beautiful we got lost in what we were doing. The moment wouldn't have happened if not for this amazing man.

Overcoming a difficult day and tricky circumstances to capture some of our favorite memories of Okinawa.

From there we stopped at Sensei Meikaru's dojo, but he was not home. He is a farmer and his wife told us he was tending the field. Although we missed him, we got to see his very beautiful dojo and some houses that he made out of stone. The children there are always happy to see Master Uezu. He gives them 1,000 Yen notes (about 9 dollars in U.S. currency).

Master Nakahodo's dojo was next, for some training and photos. As we were driving there I remember Sensei pointing and referring to a car as a "Ninja, same-same." It took us a little while, but we finally figured out he was talking about an undercover police car. Stealth, he meant. Stealth like a ninja.

A pleasant visit to the dojo of Nakahodo Sensei. Left to right: Nakahodo Sensei, Uezu Sensei, Fierro Sensei.

This was to be a full day of training as our plans for the evening included a visit to Master Shimabukuro Zenpo of Seibukan Shorinryu System. We returned to our room at 4:30 that evening. The day had already taken its toll on me and Rita. After journaling, we decided to just sit and rest our eyes for a minute. Setting two alarms for one hour, we relaxed.

Suddenly, I awoke yelling. I scared poor Rita out of her skin. Don't ask what woke me up but it was only five minutes before Sensei was to pick us up! We'd only planned on sitting and relaxing for a bit but we'd fallen asleep instead. In a panic we got up and got our things together and once more donned our Gi and raced to the lobby to meet Sensei. We immediately began practicing our forms so Uezu Sensei could see that we'd been there, ready and waiting for him.

We arrived at Shimabukuro Zenpo's dojo in time to watch some of the class before the Master came out to greet us. We discovered that Okinawa is no different from the United States...at least in one respect. Children practicing their forms on the deck can have, shall we say, a little accident. One of the students urinated on the floor in front of everyone, including Shimabukuro. It was somehow comforting to see this great master doing what all Sensei do from time to time, cleaning up after a student.

He was most courteous in his greeting and treatment of us. We worked out with his class on a couple of forms, which are similar to the ones in Isshinryu. Isshinryu incorporates parts of Shorinryu Karate and some of Gojuryu Karate as Shimabukuro Tatsuo had trained in both of these systems as well as weaponry. Zenpo Sensei's son was there and remembered me from Atlanta where I filmed the Okinawan Masters seminars in 2001.

At the end of the class I asked Master Shimabukuro to please call us a taxi to go back but he insisted on taking us back himself. We stopped by to see some of the Okinawan supermarket and shopping complex that is always a treat, and then for coffee. Master Shimabukuro bought each of us two donuts with the coffee. Remember we had been going all day and had not eaten, and we were starving. It was all we could do not to stuff both donuts in our mouths as fast as we could but we at least tried to look dignified. Donuts in Okinawa are massive and it was more than filling, odd as that sounds.

Enjoying the hospitality of Shimabukuro Zenpo Sensei. Left to right: Rita-san, Shimabukuro Sensei, Fierro Sensei.

As in so many things, training is often what occurs when you get to sit and speak with the Master. We sat with him until one in the morning learning about the politics of Okinawa and the fact that the new Governor was very supportive of karate. Master Shimabukuro had a desire for the government to help build a new Budokan (which, as I write this has become reality) that would be only for karate. The current Budokan, which I had seen in 1995, is a beautiful multi-story building that not only serves as a training center but also houses visiting martial artists. The problem was that it was a home for many arts besides karate and was often difficult to gain enough access to for long training times. A new Budokan would provide a housing and training area for karate practitioners only.

As with Master Uezu, Master Shimabukuro spoke of the need for good, basic karate. Punch, kick, block, kata, and bunkai (analysis of the moves in the kata) that form the foundation of a strong traditional style.

We learned that when he was a young boy he met Shimabukuro Tatsuo, the founder of Isshinryu Karate when he came to his home to ask his father Shimabukuro Zenryo if Zenpo could help with a demonstration. At that time, years ago, children did not train in martial arts but because Zenpo's father was a karate teacher he became a young student. After the demonstration Shimabukuro Tatsuo told his father he did well.

Okinawa and the Tenants of Isshin Ryu

One of the most memorable days of that trip was spent at Hamahiga Island. This largely untouched section of Okinawa contains houses that are three centuries old and until recently had only been accessible by boat. There we saw many sights that most people will never know about.

Visiting Okinawa is more than a journey or pilgrimage. It is, in part, a way for a practitioner to experience the homeland of karate and walk in the footsteps of those who came before. Thus, when visiting Hamahiga Island, another dream had come true since my favorite kata is Hamahiga no Tonfa.

I began to think about Shimabuku Tatsuo Sensei and how he formed our system of Okinawan Isshinryu Karate. During the struggle for survival as the war in the Pacific ravaged the island of Okinawa, Shimabuku traveled to China and there was introduced to a book called "The Bubishi," which is an encyclopedia of ancient fighting moves (some have called it "The Bible of Karate").

The Bubishi, however, also contains a series of 8 precepts or tenants. Shimabuku, being a spiritual man who was a fortune teller as well as famous martial artist, incorporated these in the Isshinryu system calling them our 8 Codes. It was the master and his codes that came to mind so vividly as we explored the island:

- A person's heart is the same as Heaven and

Earth

- The blood circulating is the same as the Moon and Sun

- The manner of drinking and spitting is either hard or soft

- A person's unbalance is the same as a weight

- The body should be able to change motion at any time

- The time to strike is when the opportunity presents itself

- The eye must see everywhere

- The ear must listen in all directions

Grandmaster Shimabuku Tatsuo Founder of Okinawan Isshinryu Karate. September 19, 1908 - May 30 1975.

As we drove around Master Uezu shared with us many stories of the early days of Isshinryu. He told us that Don Nagle was one of the U.S. Marines that participated in the day-long training sessions on a nearby island which was chosen because there were none of the poisonous indigenous Habu snakes. For me it was a special privilege to hear this story since my Sensei, Master Nick Adler, studied directly under Master Nagle. It was as if I was momentarily transported back to those early days of Isshinryu in listening to the story.

At one area of the island there was a well where fishermen would come for fresh water and at the top of the hill was a small meditation area for them to pray for rain or for a better catch. As we were absorbing that Master Uezu took my shoulders and turned me just a bit. At that angle was yet another beautiful view you could not see anywhere else. My eyes needed to see everything. It reminded me of one of our important Isshinryu precepts: "The eye sees in all directions."

"The ear listens everywhere" is another of our tenets. Sensei was driving at one point while Rita and I were chatting about different things. At one point Rita said something about me dropping down to the number two girl for Uezu but Sensei, who hadn't been in a part of our conversation, immediately said, "No. Never. Number one always."

"A person's heart is the same as heaven and earth," is a third belief of Isshinryu demonstrated to us in this trip. Sensei, in one of the many moments when he was teaching us without actually instructing, told us that the blood in our bodies circulates just like the sun and moon circulate around the Earth. Sensei said we share the same sun, moon and planet and should live together in peace. Have a good heart, he said.

Very few people have a heart as good as Uezu Sensei.

"Drinking and Spitting is either hard or soft" Yin/Yang or In/Yo You can block hard or soft to deflect. Have Balance in life "A person's unbalance is the same as a weight" In the physical and emotional sense.

We never spoke about "The time to strike is when the opportunity presents itself" or "A person should be able to change motion at any time" but those seem obvious as they are stated.

On our last day we checked out of the hotel and waited for Sensei to pick us up. All of the staff came into the lobby to hug and kiss us goodbye. They wanted us to come back again soon. They said they had seen us practice in the lobby and loved our karate. They especially liked to watch Rita-San as she repeated her forms for me. Sensei arrived and when we turned around for one last look all the staff at Hotel Kasuga had lined up outside to bow and wave to us. This continued until we were out of sight. The week had gone by so fast and we were filled with joy from the trip and sadness at leaving this beautiful place.

But, on to Japan...

We took a city tour of Tokyo after we landed and arranged to meet Ken, a gentleman from Japan who had purchased several of my "Taking Charge" TV shows. Ken was very pleasant and a pleasure to meet after the many correspondences we'd had.

The next day Rita and I took a train back to Asakasa which is an area of shops and a mixture of old and new Japan. We had arranged to meet Ken for lunch while we were there and he helped us to read some signs and find an Internet Cafe. After he left we took some time to send messages home, but it was really funny because one little mistake and the keyboard turned to Japanese!

The next day we took a train to see the Big Buddha in Kamakura. Again, it was Rita's first time but not mine. Even so, the sight of that massive statue will never cease to amaze me.

Finally I got to see it in sunshine. Our tour guide for this day trip was Haruko. Her husband was a sports writer for the newspapers so we spoke a lot about karate. We found out that in Japan, Sumo wrestling (not karate) is the popular national sport.

Another thing our guide taught us is that there are different ways to bow to people. The bow is part of polite culture in Japan. You bow when you meet someone, or say goodbye, or interact in a formal way. However, not all bows are appropriate. They have specific measurements for specific situations:

15 degrees to a colleague

30 degrees to a superior (a senpai, sensei, boss, etc.)

45 degrees to a VIP

and jokingly Haruko said 90 degrees when a husband comes home late and bows to his wife!

An excellent view of Kamakura.

In Kamakura we also took a rickshaw tour of the area. It was a cold day so we were both placed on warming pads with blankets. It is definitely a weird feeling when the man who pulls the rickshaw lifts it up. He assured us he was strong and we should not worry but it did take a bit for trust to follow especially on some of the steeper hills.

It was amazing to see the strength in this slender man. We saw two houses not far from one another and were told it had been one house and an earthquake split it in two, so the people simply made them into two separate houses. He told us about some of the people in the areas he took us to as well.

As I watched him I noticed his stances. It was like he was performing martial arts in his work. He would start out in a deep zenkutsu dachi and then move along in a comfortable stance reverting back to the longer one when he needed to start or stop, but it was always a good stance as if he had trained under a master rickshaw driver.

In a culture such as Japan, or Okinawa, martial arts is everywhere. It is part of life.

A fantastic rickshaw experience under the care of a master driver.

Part 3 – Here and Now

Chapter 14 – An Unexpected Promotion

Sometime in March or April 2014 we heard that there was a group of Isshinryu Martial Artists in Thunder Bay, Canada hosting a large expo to honor our friend, Hanshi Al Mady, who had been going there for the past thirty years to teach. We began to inquire about it as Sensei and I thought it would be so nice to attend this event for Master Mady.

We were put in touch with Kyoshi Susan Baldassi. From my first conversation with her I was hooked. I knew she was a person I could relate to who shared not only Isshinryu Karate but the more spiritual aspect that I too had been developing over the years.

We were eager to participate in the expo at the Thunder Bay Recreation Center but realized the airfare was too much for us at the time. Sadly, we decided not to go, until Susan convinced us to teach and she would take care of the airfare. How exciting to know we were going to Canada and going to teach as well. I was surprised when both of us were asked to teach five sessions of our own. I might have expected that kind of request for Adler Sensei, but I was always one to teach a single session at best.

Adler Sensei was teaching combat techniques, bo, sai, kata and speed drills. I was teaching tekko, tonfa, Wansu Kata, blocking drills and energy work. Together Hanshi Mady, Hanshi Adler and I were to take a Q &A session. This was the first time I had so many sessions and I was thrilled.

After checking immigration standards we realized carrying weapons to Canada was going to be a problem. So, we looked into shipping our weapons. Evidently you cannot do that either. Who knew they were so strict? I had been to Canada but always as a tourist so I never encountered these issues. When you think of Canada from the United States you hardly even consider it another country because we're so close, but here we were, with no way to bring our weapons through border security.

We were told there would be plenty of weapons for us to use and not to worry. I figured we could make do with that. Then I was told that one of the black belts, Rob Prdn, had made tekkos for that part of my session. The tekko is a "fist-loaded" weapon very similar to brass knuckles. I looked at a picture of them that he had posted and realized they would never fit my hands, and even though they might be well made they weren't the right style for what I wished to teach.

My tekko of choice looked like a weapon and because of that I wouldn't be able to travel with it. However, there is another weapon called a chizenkun bo. chizenkun bo are short slightly rounded sticks that were originally used as floats on fishing nets and also for gathering up the net and scraping off barnacles. These short sticks have a center string to put a finger through and the rounded wood fits into the hand with just enough protrusion on both ends to make for good grappling, palm blocks, and finger strikes (nukite) when rotated to point out. With a little creativity, I took the strings out of my chizenkun bo and placed them inside my shoes...as shoe trees!

Problem solved. Now there was no reason for our friends to the North to keep me from bringing them across the border, and more than that I would have the right style of weapon I needed to teach the forms I wanted to teach.

On May 16th we flew to Canada from Newark Airport and arrived in Toronto on time. At Immigration we were asked all of the usual questions and my heart began to thump a little louder. What if they asked about my shoes? We were asked why we were coming to Canada. I replied we are going to an expo. When they asked where we were staying...I didn't have the address. I told the border agent again that we were going to an expo and produced the flyer, with the address and all the information on it. Then he asked us why we were going there. I said, to teach.

It's a little known fact that there are very few reasons that will allow you to enter another country. Sightseeing and shopping are two of the biggest. You can get into almost any country if you tell them you're there to spend money. If I'd said to the nice border patrol agents that we were there to do some shopping we probably would have gotten right in. Instead, I had to be honest and tell them we were there to teach at an expo.

So then, the agent asked, "Where are your working papers?"

What working papers? We were helping a friend. That wasn't good enough. He asked how much we were being paid to teach and I told him nothing, it's a favor to a friend. I figured that would settle it. Surely we didn't need papers if we weren't getting paid!

I was wrong. That only made it worse.

The agent asked who paid for our tickets, and of course we explained that our friend at the expo had paid for the tickets. In that case, the agents said, we were being paid because we had received a monetary benefit.

Well, what should have been a simple trip into Canada turned into a two hour ordeal for us. It involved several phone calls back and forth with Kyoshi Susan Baldassi at the expo, and even when she capitulated and told the agent that we wouldn't teach, they still insisted that we couldn't come into the country.

The agents scoured their rule books and found one tiny loophole. The Thunder Bay Recreation Center is a non-profit organization. No work papers required for non-profit organizations. So finally, we were on our way. We got to Thunder Bay the same day, even though all that time was lost.

Saturday morning arrived with opening ceremony introductions and the Mayoral Award and then on to teaching. Adler Sensei always does a great job and anyone who ever trains with him can certainly attest to that. I didn't have anywhere near his seminar teaching experience but I gave it my all. My first seminar was a seven step blocking drill which Sensei had developed. I was so confident when I said I would teach it because I have had good success with it at my dojo even though it is a difficult drill to teach and perform. Sensei pointed out that I didn't have a partner and wondered how I would be able to teach it. I said I would do fine. As they say, famous last words, right?

There was a red/white belt who looked energetic and strong so I asked him to work with me. Initially I teach this as two separate kata and then put it together so that's what I did that day.

When the students were ready to team up I paired off with one of the men I thought was good and we demonstrated a few of the moves. Eventually we were able to get through all seven steps of the drill. By the time the session was about over Sensei came over to see how we were doing and I had my partner demonstrate with another man. I told them they had to make me look good and they sure did. I was so proud of them.

For the next session I taught Wansu Bunkai. Just before the end of the session a reporter came in and Kyoshi Baldassi introduced me and requested I perform a takedown technique for the reporter's photographer. We moved a mat over and I asked a gentleman who had really good energy if he could fall and he said yes. You might be surprised how important that is, and how much time we practice just falling in the martial arts. The photographer took two photos and the next day we were on the front page of the sports section of the Canadian paper, the only photo from the seminars.

Hamahiga No Tonfa came next. It is my favorite weapons form and I was so happy to see how much the students liked it as well. That was followed by tekkos shortly after.

I loved the energy of the students at this expo and it in turn energized me. One of the courses I taught was about energy and Ki. There was a large spiritual group who participated and I want to say this did intimidate me a bit when I spoke about the energy of the crystal as a way to demonstrate Ki and when I led a guided meditation as well. At the end there was dead silence in the room. Can I tell you what a horrible feeling it was! I must have done something wrong, I thought. Then everyone started to talk and tell me their experiences with meditation. There was a couple there who I could feel were very spiritual but also I felt a mixture of emotions emanating from them. Later we were able to speak and it turned out she was having some doubts and the meditation helped her to be more focused. I will say by the next day there were more smiles than before. Good energy makes a great difference.

Fierro Sensei leading a tekkos seminar.

That evening there was a banquet where we were awarded a very nice certificate for teaching. When it was Sensei's turn to receive his certificate, he asked if he could say something. I thought he was going to speak about Hanshi Mady and was shocked when he began to speak about me and my accomplishments. My first thought was that someone complained about me and he needed to defend me, but he was in fact very proud of me and announced my promotion to 9th dan.

I felt as if I couldn't breathe. I could not believe what I had just heard.

About two months prior, Grandmaster Uezu had recognized Adler Sensei as 10th Dan a rank which he had also received three years earlier from Grandmaster Harold Mitchum. I had been an 8th Dan for the past ten years. Master Uezu used to tell me I should be a 9th Dan but I always told him my Sensei is 9th so I can only be 8th.

So, imagine how the tears fell when this happened at the expo. It was a total shock and such a surprise that I could not even stand up. He had to walk to the table where I was still sitting with my mouth open in amazement. I finally stood and gave him a hug and told him thanks. I don't think I even remembered to bow. He motioned for me to turn around and the entire room was standing and applauding. Sensei had totally taken me by surprise.

Adler Sensei, Mady Sensei, and Fierro Sensei during the 9th Dan promotional banquet.

Around the time prior to Adler Sensei's promotion

to 10th dan I was at his home helping him and he asked me to bring in a bag from the other room. I did and he began looking through various obi (belts). He pulled out one of his red belts and said it had belonged to Grandmaster Nagle. He asked me to try it on which I did and he said it was a little short. I said, "Who else could fit into it?" That day as I was leaving he gave me the obi and said, "Take it home. When the time is right you can wear this." Talk about ecstatic!

Back to Canada. Sensei pulled a different red belt out of his bag and said, "Here, wear this tomorrow." It was a little longer than Nagle Sensei's belt, and a better fit. It was one of Adler Sensei's own belts.

As soon as the banquet and congratulations ended I excused myself and asked Sensei's permission to call my dojo brothers, Tommy May and Ray Bradley, who had also received promotions that day (even though they couldn't attend in-person). Tommy and Ray helped me immensely along the way so it is a pleasure that we could all share this honor. In my heart I wished Rick Adler had been part of this moment but sadly family and career obligations – as well as distance – just got in the way.

I received many texts, phone calls and emails of congratulations. Some from other countries yet each holding special place in my heart. For people I love and respect to recognize my accomplishment meant the world to me.

Soon I became known as the highest ranking woman in Isshinryu Karate and was recognized by just about every major Isshinryu association as such. There is, however, one woman in Rochester, NY, by the name of Cindy Jones who should be recognized. She is with the Isshinryu World Karate Association and she received her 9th Dan before me. So, when I was introduced at the Isshinryu Masters Symposium in Ohio as the highest ranking woman I had to speak up and mention Cindy. Master Chuck Wallace from the IWKA was present and it was important for me to be honest.

Later when I spoke with Master Wallace he put his arm on my shoulder and said, "Marilyn, you deserve everything that is said about you." What an honor to hear that from him. and quite a relief.

Chapter 15 – Concluding Thoughts

I tell you these stories so you can see how often things work out. Even the impossible can become reality, so if I can do it you can too.

All of us have circumstances in our lives both good and bad. They don't have to define us. We were given the gift of freewill, and that means we have the ability to move forward and redefine our lives. We need to grow, we need to learn, and we need to keep re-inventing ourselves. Trust your heart to help you along the way. You will know the right course to take when you learn to trust yourself. Be YOU – be your best each day and look for ways to be better. Accomplish your goals and search for new ones.

Remember, life is not a destination. Life is a journey. Make yours a good one.

Consider the following:

• HAPPINESS COMES FROM WITHIN - No one gives it to you and no one can take it from you without your permission.

• FOLLOW YOUR HEART - You know what the right choice is, trust yourself and don't give in to doubts.

• BELIEVE IN YOURSELF - If you want it you can do it. Make a plan and stick to it. You are worthy.

• WHO ARE YOU? - You are more than a parent, child, job, boss, worker. We all wear many hats and are many things to different people. That is not who we are. You were born with a sole purpose and once you lock into what that is you will be on the right path.

• MEDITATE - Empty your mind and be open to possibilities. Answers come when you least expect them. Challenges teach us lessons so use them to discover your true self.

• LESSONS COME IN MANY FORMS - Some good and some not so good, but they do not need to define who we are. Change your thoughts and you just might change your result.

• REMOVE DOUBT - Make a difference. Figure out your sole purpose and make a mark that will last.

Part 4 – Articles

Chapter 16 – Uezu Angi – A Man with a Big Heart

In the process of working on this book I discovered the following article which I had written and submitted to a magazine on April 25, 1987. I know this because it is on the last page of the following typewritten story. What I do not know is if it was ever published, and if so, which of the magazines I had been writing for actually printed it. I thought this might be something you would enjoy reading as well.

Master Uezu was with Hanshi Adler and myself for one of our events and this is the result of an interview I had with him at that time. It is exactly as I had written it with no changes. Pictures have been collected and added specifically for this book.

Uezu Angi ...... a man with a big heart
by Marilyn Fierro

Tucked within the depths of this gentle man's soul lies the essence which is known as "The Spirit of Isshinryu Karate." Isshinryu means "One Heart Way" and Master Uezu Angi is certainly a man with a big heart. He spent 20 years training with Isshinryu Founder and Father-in-Law, Master Shimabuku Tatsuo, before his death in 1975 and has continued to train and perfect the system he loves. Now, at the age of 52 he seems as fast, strong and tireless as ever. He may claim that time has slowed him down, but watching him throw a flying side kick to the head of his opponent or execute one of his sport kick moves lends little truth to that fact.

Home or away, Master Uezu spends three hours daily at Isshinryu training. "For good karate you must sweat", claims Master Uezu. "The student may not understand this at first, but the instructor knows and can see the progress brought out by this effort". Isshinryu has been referred to as a Masters system, possibly because Shimabuku Tatsuo encompassed some of the most difficult and higher forms from Shorinryu (Chotoku Kiyan and Choki Motobu) and Gojuryu (Gogen Miyagi) systems when creating his style. Additionally, through his studies with Taira Shinken, Okinawan weapons forms were incorporated within the boundary of this empty hand style.

Master Uezu recently spent five days with the Nick Adler's Centurions schools on Long Island, NY. During that time he offered the following information about the weapons forms of Isshinryu Karate:

BO - Originally carried on a daily basis by farmers and towns people as a way to transport food, clothing or water. The bo easily adapted to a fighting situation by allowing extra reach. A good Bo man was fast, accurate and difficult to approach.

TOKOMINE NO KUN - This form comes from the Shorinryu system. The name Tokomine is the family name of the man who created the form. No Kun means my Bo (or Of Bo).

Urashi Bo - The form originated 300 years ago and is named after the village of the same name.

SHISHI NO KUN NO DAI - Also known as Master Bo, this translates into Shishi (teacher) no kun (bo) Dai (big). The origin of this form is unknown.

BO/BO KUMITE - A form of one step sparring bo against bo, containing a series of ten techniques, which gives the practitioner an opportunity to work blocking and striking movements in a pre-arranged form. Although reality dictates more strikes to the hands , the bo/bo kumite movements are to the weapon for practical purposes.

SAI - was originally part of the Nunte Bo, a gaff used to hook fish into the boat. When removed it was adapted by policemen as a weapon to defend against the sword. Carried in sets of three, it was used to block the blade while the other Sai stabbed hand or body. The third Sai could be used as a throwing weapon.

KUSANKU SAI - Kusanku is a Chinese name. Kusanku was a guard at the castle gate. He was also Buken – a karate teacher of Bo Jutsu, a defensive weapons system. It was thought he developed this Sai form although many also believed it was simply a Sai exercise developed from the hand form of the same name. The original version had no kicks, but Master Shimabuku added kicks in 1967.

SAI CHATAN YARA - Yara is the man's name and Chatan is his town and Sai is his weapon. It is commonly believed to be a Sai form developed by Yara, however, Master Uezu was told by Master Shimabuku that when Yara came to Shuri Castle he met Kusanku who then became his teacher. Kusanku taught him the Sai form and subsequently named it after his student. In 1960 Taira Shinken came to Master Uezu's home. He spent ten days with him working on the proper execution of this form.

BO/SAI KUMITE - The concept is essentially the same as Bo/Bo kumite except the Sai is substituted for one bo. This ten move exercise ends with the Sai person removing his opponent's bo and maintaining control over him.

TONFA - is the handle on a rice grinding machine and was easily removed to become a strong weapon for blocking, striking and covering.

Although used in pairs when doing kata, its spinning action makes it just as functional alone. This is the reason that many modern day police departments have adapted the Tonfa as part of their daily equipment. The form Master Shimabuku added to Isshinryu was taught to him by Macabe (I may have that wrong due to his accent when speaking to me).

NUNCHAKU - was a farm tool used as an agricultural flail. Isshinryu's Nunchaku form is a Kihon or Basic form demonstrating blocks, strikes and covering moves.

KAMA - Isshinryu does not have a Kama form. Kama is, however, a traditional Okinawan weapon used for cutting rice in the field. During the Japanese takeover of Okinawa the Samurai used to control the people by throwing fish nets over them, therefore, many of the movements in Kama kata depict the defensive cutting away of these nets. Master Uezu was quick to point out that "Kama's main use is to block or punch with the handle, when striking with the blade end it is always turned so that the back of the blade becomes the striking surface." Okinawan people do not like to kill anyone. They would much rather disarm and incapacitate an opponent. This is most evident by the fact that all Okinawan kata, weapons or empty hand begin with a block.

The best way to perfect your use of a weapon, according to Master Uezu, is to work with the desired weapon in the following manner:

BASIC TECHNIQUES - Setting up a series of basic techniques which are based upon the movements within the kata. This gives the student a concept of the weapon without having to memorize an actual form at first.

SPEED TRAINING - Working individual moves in a series with maximum speed. This allows the flow and continuity of movement.

SWING TRAINING - This refers mainly to the use of the Bo. Many people do not realize the angle at which a Bo is swung will change the desired result. For example a rib strike executed at an angle rather than straight across will have less power than a direct hit. This is much the same as a punch which merely grazes the body. It is also necessary when swinging the Bo to work on a push/pull type basis with both hands working to create maximum power.

BLOCKING TRAINING - Working the various blocks with your weapon and using your partner to practice application of these blocks. Using the Bo as the attacking weapon, work a series of attacks in which you must first block and then counter the attack.

PUNCHING TRAINING - Practicing the various strikes with your weapon, first in the air and then on a more solid surface such as a bag or tree. Many weapons will react differently when struck on a firm surface. The Nunchaku is a prime example of this, if you chose an open weapon strike the angle with which you hit a solid surface determines the angle with which your weapon will return to you. It takes considerable practice to gain mastery under these conditions. Sai and Tonfa practice include flipping the edge out and back. When connecting with a solid surface you will easily recover the weapon without injury to yourself. When punching with the Bo the weapon is rotated so that It becomes locked into the strike. By using a twisting motion with the wrists and following the body line the practitioner maintains control and generates power. With a shorter weapon it is necessary to lock the closed weapon along the forearm when punching.

FOCUS TRAINING - Is aiming your strikes at a target to develop KIME. Use a target such as a can or a leaf to improve aim. With the Tonfa, practice being able stop and control the weapon at the target without touching it.

Kata is an important part of weapons training. It is within these formalized movements that the legacy of the masters have been placed. Each form was handed down to us by a particular master with the direct purpose of teaching us a specific set of fighting moves. The execution of your kata is an expression of your understanding of this bunkai (the meaning behind a specific move). Bunkai, or correct application of a kata move, is evident through a properly executed form. Therefore, practice of kata is essential to the understanding of individual moments. In viewing forms, especially in competition, it becomes obvious to the trained eyes as to whether or not the practitioner comprehends his or her weapons.

According to Uezu Angi, Master Shimabuku Tatsuo likened the teaching of kata to the creation of a fine statue. The statue passes through four stages. Starting as a raw element, it begins to take shape, eventually becoming more recognizable, and, finally when polished and completed, becomes a work of art.

ARA KEZURI- (beginning) The first stage where the student is taught the rudiments of the kata and is expected to remember the moves in their proper sequence. The Karateka at this stage is like the raw material of the statue.

With continued practice the form begins to take shape and the student enters NAKA KEZURI (middle). The student is at the halfway point, the kata has form but lacks Kime (focus).

Finally the fine details of the kata are perceived. The student no longer thinks about which move comes next and thus can attain Kime. He is 80 percent of the way, the statue is finely detailed and he has attained HOSO KEZURI (top).

With constant practice (Usually 3 years on one form alone) the student will pull himself beyond the top to reach SHIYAGI. At this stage the Karateka is in harmony both physically and mentally. He has achieved inner power (ki), he has come 100 percent of the way, beyond the physical into the spiritual. The statue is complete, it is polished and has become a work of art.

The more you work you weapon, via forms or

individual movements, through practice with a partner and against other weapons, the more understanding you will attain. The road to Shiyagi is yours, it takes dedication, sweat, hard work and most of all heart. As Master Uezu says "for good karate you must have heart." It is heart that has made him the major representative of Isshinryu Karate today and it is this spirit of "The one heart way" that he passes on to all who wish to learn.

Picture Tour of Uezu Angi Sensei

9		29	
10		30	
11		31	
12	PLEASE BOOK MAKE		
13	M	33	
14		34	
15		35	
16		36	
17		37	
18		38	
19		39	
20		40	

Honoring the wishes of Uezu Sensei as best as possible by including the following images and moments of his life.

Uezu Sensei poses at the age of 19. Left to Right: Uezu Anyu (Cousin), Uezu Angi, Toguchi Soko, Kotani Ryomei

June of 1956. Uezu Angi (21 years old) with wife Yukiko.

"Kyan Dojo and Home, Water Tank (Dream Mizugami). My Wife Yukiko."

"Grandmaster Shimabuku 3 Daughters: Haruko, Yukiko, Matsuko"

Home photo of Master Uezu in the 1950s.

In front of Agena Dojo in 1960.

Security guard at Camp Foster in 1963.

"December 6 1964, Kiyan Home and Dojo Party"

Shimabuku Tatsuo Sensei with Uechi Kanei Sensei.

Student demonstration lineup in 1965. Uezu Sensei far right.

Board breaking demonstration in 1972.

A different kind of board breaking in 1973

Side kick to Joe Jennings in 1978.

A favorite moment and lasting memory. Uezu Sensei's famous smile, and a feeling of approval from him.

Chapter 17 – The Limitless Spirit of the Martial Arts

This article was first printed in 1982 in The Taekwondo Times. It is reprinted here with permission, unaltered from its original state for your enjoyment and consideration.

"Perfection doesn't have limits. Perfect speed, my son, is being there." So says Master Chang to his student Jonathan in Richard Bach's story of Jonathan Livingston Seagull. We are limited only by that which we cannot conceive. In the time before automobiles, airplanes and nuclear power, we were limited by what we could dream up. Now, our horizons have been extended past those concepts and onto limitless horizons.

As a martial artist the "I can't" should not exist for, if we choose to do so, we can simply take the necessary steps to attain our goals.

How many times have we read of the accomplishments of martial artists who are disabled in some manner? Were they truly disabled? No, because they took the necessary steps to overcome their physical limitations. What about the martial artist whose negative thoughts prevented him from earning rank, winning trophies or executing a perfect side kick? Is this individual not the handicapped one? By replacing negative thoughts with positive ones, by setting goals and working toward achieving them, the possibilities are limitless.

When Bill "Superfoot" Wallace was told his knee injury would prevent him from training as a martial artist, was that the end for him? No! He took the steps necessary to develop left leg kicks, strengthened his almost useless right leg and went on to become the undefeated champion of full contact karate.

The perfection is in setting goals, achieving them and resetting goals. It is in the striving to be even better. The archer who learns to hit the bullseye 100% of the time, now strives to center his arrow, and then to split the arrow, again and again, an infinitesimal number of times. There is no end to this accomplishment. It goes on and on as long as the idea exists, as long as there is a whole there will always be a piece of it that needs work. This, then, is the perfection – it lies within the deed itself and the constant training needed to improve upon the tiniest detail.

We have a conscious and a subconscious mind. Our very conscious thoughts act upon our subconscious mind to form a pattern for us. Thus a negative thought will be reinforced and bring into action a great deal of negativity. This reflects into our world as the inability to attain success, the non-belief in ourselves and others, and ultimately, ill health.

On the other hand, a positive thought creates within us a positive mental attitude. Now we have the ability to attain anything to which we put our minds.

The key to this is simple: We cannot deny the existence of negativity, but we can see it for what it is and allow it to slide by. We need not accept negativity! Replace negative thoughts with positive ones and create for yourself a winning attitude. Doctor Maxwell Maltz, in his book, PSYCHOCYBERNETICS, details the use of mental imagery to create this positive attitude.

Controlled scientific studies were conducted on tennis players of a similar skill level. Four groups were formed. One was to play tennis each day, one was to watch films and use visualization techniques, the third was to do nothing, and the fourth was to both study and play tennis. As would be expected the group which did nothing showed a marked decline in skill level and the group which played showed a slight increase in skill. Unexpectedly, the group which used visualization also showed a small increase of skill level and the group which did both were able to demonstrate a marked increase. This type of survey was repeated with martial artists and the results were reported by Tom Seabourne in KICK ILLUSTRATED, September, 1983.

Time spent mentally practicing your technique can and will be rewarded with perfection of that technique. Mike Stone's current motivational seminars contain within them this same idea. Here he stresses the idea of knowing you are a winner, seeing yourself with the trophy and accepting nothing less as your reality. Ninety-three consecutive recorded wins proves this idea to be true for Mister Stone.

We have the ability to be whatever we wish to be. There are no limits. Simply conceive the idea, set the goal, take the steps and be there. But, you must BELIEVE.

"To fly as fast as thought to anywhere that is, you must begin by knowing you have already arrived." – Richard Bach.

Marilyn Fierro

Chapter 18 - Exploring the Spiritual and its Connection to Karate

As I mentioned earlier in this book, I don't remember much of my life before the eighth grade. What I do remember, quite vividly, are my dreams. I called them my floating dreams. I would go on a magic carpet ride, sometimes without the carpet, to visit places from all over the world. It was wonderful and exciting and I could not wait to get to bed at night. After a while I began to encounter a darker side that scared me. At that point I did not want to go to sleep and when I did I would complain that my blankets were not tight enough.

One night my step-dad tried to assuage my fears by tying rope around my bed when I went to sleep. That turned out to be the best night's sleep I had in a long time. When I awoke in the morning I carefully slid out of bed so as to not disturb the ropes on the covers, and continued to use them for many nights to come.

It was not until I became an adult that I realized what had been happening. I now believe that children are born with an understanding about spirituality, knowing they have a connection to everything. What I had been doing as a child was astral projection – at that time I had the ability to leave my body and venture to different places. It is much the same as the stories you hear from people who have died on the operating table but know everything that went on around them before they returned to life. Our soul, the essence of who we are, is connected to our bodies by a silver cord so it is possible for us to leave our body for short times and return safely. What I did not understand at the time, but I do now, is that we need to be protected before trying these kinds of spiritual endeavors. When we open up like this we need to ask for protection first. There is a Universal force that most of us call God. It does not matter what you want to call this force or what your religious beliefs are. What matters is that you can recognize its existence.

When I meditate, before opening myself to anything, I ask the following:

"Dear God in Heaven please send down a beautiful white light filled with love, wisdom, understanding, perfect health, and balance. Let no negativity enter in and only the purest most positive entities, angels, arch angels, and guides advise and protect me. I ask this humbly and sincerely and without reservation."

I then visualize a white light of protection entering in through the top of my head, through the crown chakra, and move down through each of the remaining six chakras throughout my body then emerge to surround me like a protective cocoon with that perfect Universal light of protection. All of this is done mentally and can be used anytime you need protection or to open up through meditation.

I believe all healings and information come from a higher source. Please remember as well to offer your thanks for all things seen and unseen in your life.

One day when I was young and still riding a tricycle I was in the court yard of our apartment complex trying to see how fast I could peddle. My legs were moving as fast as they could, so fast that I did not see a crack in the cement. The next thing I knew I was airborne. I literally flew high enough into the air that I was upside down. I remember thinking that I was going to land on my head and even today I remember seeing the ground coming at me.

Suddenly the tricycle righted itself and I was fine. I doubt I even told my parents. It was not until I met Doctor William Bezman and began a journey within that I learned the truth about what really happened.

Everything happens for a reason. There are no coincidences and we each evolve in our own way. I would like, now, to share with you some of the occurrences that brought me to the stage of investigating the psychic, spiritual and energetic realm and eventually connecting it to the martial arts. In truth it is a simple path and would have happened to me even if I had discovered jogging instead of karate. The results would have been the same.

While I was still searching for myself through tennis, yoga, and so forth I also became involved with helping at cancer care functions. One day there was a fundraiser where a mentalist had been brought in to perform readings. Each of us wrote two questions on index cards prior to the session. I was such a nonbeliever at that time but I decided to play along anyway. The mentalist made a show of putting coins and cotton over his eyes and then wrapping a bandana around the entire thing. He would draw cards from the audience at random and then answer the questions printed on them. I felt they were all pre-written answers and did not believe any of it. Then he pulled a card and said "Oh, this person is a nonbeliever." I thought, yeah well so am I. He went on to answer the other questions on the card that I knew for sure were mine. That certainly gave me food for thought.

It jogged something in me and I began to search for more. I started by listening to some meditation tapes by a man named Dick Sutphen, he actually did one about being a martial artist and achieving goals. He had also written a book called *You Were Born To Be Together* which explored the theory of past lives. I found that interesting as I always felt that people who came into our lives were there for a reason.

I continued to explore other avenues. One theory that is difficult to grasp is that life is like a multi-dimensional chess board with similar lives happening all at once. It is one thing to think about the immensity of the Universe but to think all levels could even be happening almost simultaneously on the Earth plane is a bit overwhelming.

I do believe there is more than what is obvious. I used to have a poster by Dr. Wayne Dyer that said something to the effect, "it is not a matter of seeing is believing it is more that if you believe it you will see it." Our mind is creative so think positive and you will attract more positive experiences into your life.

Energy is strong. Just think about the power of electricity yet it is something you cannot see. I demonstrate that with a simple Kinesiology experiment using thought to either strengthen or weaken a person. It is also the way I can move a crystal with my mind. Actually Semyon Davidovich Kirlian and his wife worked together with high voltage photography taking thirty years to develop their equipment and study electro-photography. Using Kirlian photography you can actually see the energy emitted by people in different circumstances. In one experiment two people would speak and begin to argue while their index fingers are facing each other a few inches apart. Initially you can see the energy movement between the fingers and as an argument ensues the energy of the person winning begins to invade the space of the other person and the other person's energy field pulls away. Similarly Kirlian photography was used to film a martial artist punching. First a basic strike and then one where Ki was extended and you could actually see the energy extend to a far greater distance.

We are made of energy. There is a field around our bodies called the auric field. It is always emitting energy and can extend away from our bodies. Did you ever notice how many people want to be near you when you are in a good mood and how many ignore you or even back away when you are in a foul mood? It is because in a good or happy mood your auric field extends out while in a bad or unhappy mood it is pulled in. People can pick up bad vibrations without realizing it and a person who was in a good mood riding a train home from work for example may arrive home already in a grumpy mood. People who are not attuned to energy fields will still react and not even realize they are sensing discomfort and why. It is a warning to avoid situations when they do not feel right. It is also the same feeling you get when you know someone has been in your room, it's more than something out of place.

This is the same energy I found to be most effective in my self-defense programs as I truly believe I have prevented conflict by the energy I presented at the time. But be forewarned. By using energy – the power of thought – you are now accountable for your actions. Many people will say whatever goes around comes around, but it is more than that. Whatever we put out returns to us tenfold. Therefore, now that you understand how our thoughts can generate positive or negative reactions in ourselves or others be careful not to abuse this power.

One day I read that Dick Sutphen would be in New York. Terry Maccarrone and I had always spoken about these spiritual happenings and our beliefs so I spoke to him about going to see Sutphen and we decided to go together. I no longer remember all the details of the seminar but two things stand out in my mind. We did a lot of meditating and one exercise was for us to meet our spirit guide. We all have a guide, or an angel if you prefer, who is with us and trying to help guide us on this difficult earthly plane. It was a good meditation but felt funny... I don't know how to explain it other than to say it was a different experience for me and I received a guide with a very common name. I did not believe my result and although I tried to meditate on him nothing seemed to work so I eventually just stopped.

The second thing happened at the end of the seminar. I had been taping most of it throughout the day and left my recorder taping while everyone joined hands and began to chant ohm, ohm, bringing up the vibrational energy of the room and all around ius. Later when I tried to listen to what I had recorded, things that were there before were all erased! You could argue that it kept running so long that it overwrote itself, but that does not explain the tapes I had made and taken out of the recorder. Those too were blank.

Years later I learned that Dick Sutphen was going to hold another seminar in Sedona Arizona where the energy is extremely strong due to the vortexes in the area. It was around the time of our normal vacation so I asked my husband if we could go to the Grand Canyon that year and attend the seminar. He agreed and plans were made. We booked flights from JFK in New York to Las Vegas and then we were to transfer to a connecting flight that would bring us to the canyon area. When we landed in Vegas they told us to get our bags to bring to another terminal. We were confused but of course we did as we were told. That flight was on a small plane and after checking in, they weighed our bags and then asked us to get on the scale. Our plane had five or possibly seven seats. Ralph and I were across from one another in the middle, our younger son, Steven, sat in the front with the pilot and Michael sat alone in the tail. It was hot on the ground but once we had balanced the plane out the pilot assured us it would be cooler as we rose. The air came from side vent windows like on the old VW bug before AC.

It was an interesting flight over Hoover Dam and into the Grand Canyon itself before landing on one of the rims. If you have never been to the Grand Canyon put it on your bucket list today. I do not think there is anything more humbling than to realize how small we are in the scheme of things. The energy of the canyon is palpable and changes almost from moment to moment. A couple of days there was not nearly enough to absorb it all but it certainly did not prepare us for the red rocks of Sedona and the energy you feel there.

A vortex has been described as an area of spiraling energy. It is something difficult to explain but if you are open enough you can feel different energies in the various areas. You need a good guide book to find the vortexes and of course you must have an open mind. Meditating at a vortex brings forth interesting thoughts and feelings. As I said not everyone is open to these feelings and not everyone will experience them. But I would like to share a little of mine.

I believe it was Boynton Canyon where the negative energy was so strong it felt like a weight on me and I wanted to rush everyone out of it. No one else felt like that. In fact they seemed to be enjoying the walk. At one time we were at the top of a mountain and I sat down and began to meditate. Soon I had the vision of an Indian Chief who was with the Chiefs of many tribes. Most of the other Chiefs wanted to go to war but he did not. Toward the end of my meditation I felt extremely sad that I could not stop the war and began to feel as if I could just jump off that mountain and fly. I had to press my back hard against the rock behind me as the pull to jump became so strong. I realized I was feeling the Chief's energy, not my own, and that the Chief actually jumped off that cliff rather than see the war.

Later I saw a post card in the store with a photo of a Chief on it and it was exactly like the one in my meditation. I tell you this because I want you to be aware of the power of meditation and different energies on people.

After spending days of meditation at the seminars and then a day walking through the vortexes it was time for our last seminar. We were to do a meditation to find our spirit guide, quite similar to the exercise I had done years ago. I was so tired that as I began to meditate I fell sound asleep. The next thing I heard Dick saying, it was time to come back from the meditation. Everyone was all excited about their guides and there I was with none.

The next exercise was for us to pair off with someone we do not know and we were to work on telemetry. Telemetry is picking up energy from a piece of metal that a person wears or normally carries. I was now paired with a gentleman who handed me his wedding ring. Well, at least I know he is married. I tried to read the ring but nothing came. Finally, I tried to ask for the guide from that time in the New York City meditation. I found myself at the bottom of a spiral staircase filled with spider webs. I had to clear away the webs and by the time I got to the top there were all kinds of locks and chains on the door. I finally got it open and there he was. A man in a long robe with his hands on his hips who sayid, "Oh, you need me so now you come."

I could hear in the background it was time to leave the meditation, so I kept apologizing to my guide and promised to work with him and thanked him for helping me. But, I said I have to come back and say something more for this man other than the fact he is married. I was given information that he did not have children and they were looking for a new house and was given three numbers. When I came out of the meditation I told him all of that plus the three numbers of the house. He did indeed look at a house as I described and the three numbers were correct but in reverse. Wow. Unfortunately for me he did not get any images or thoughts from what I had given him to read.

A more interesting meditation that occurred on this trip was when we were asked to go back to a past life and discover why it is we do what we do. I was teaching martial arts by then but it was not my career and I was still looking to return to working as a Histologist. I had no idea what to expect so went with the flow of what I was receiving in the meditation. The realization of its martial arts connection did not hit me till quite a bit later. It is one thing to think about something but it is quite another to learn through meditation. When you are in the meditation it is as if you are there. If, perchance, you actually go to an important place or time the emotions you experience become quite real. In this meditation I was the son of a king. I lived in Castle on a hill and had a good life. I could actually feel the joy of my life in that time. We were then asked to move to an important event in that lifetime and I saw that kingdom was being attacked and everyone had to go to battle. Being the King's son it was my job to lead the troops. But, I was terrified (I could actually feel the fear in my own body as I experienced this meditation). When it was time for the battle I basically ran away and rode my horse to the top of the hill and just watched what was going on down below. I felt terrible knowing I was a coward. What would I tell my father?

My distress felt so real to me in this meditation I cannot even begin to tell you. In the meditation I suddenly felt the presence of the attacking leader on the same hill not far from me. He saw me, and I saw him at the same time. He began to charge toward me and I knew with certainty I was about to die. I sat frozen to the saddle and I could feel the muscles tighten beneath me as my horse felt the anticipation of the conflict. I don't know if it was bravery or fear but at the last second I brought up my spear and shifted to my right just as he was about to run me through and instead he ran into my spear. I had killed the leader and essentially ended the battle. As I rode back to the castle with the remainder of our troops I felt miserable. They considered me a hero and I was just a coward – I knew it in the depth of my being and felt the sadness and guilt for all of it.

At that point the meditation was ending and we were asked to look ahead in that time for a happier moment. I found myself teaching the troops how to shift and use angles. I was happy as I no longer had to use it in battle but could teach others. As we came out of the entire meditation I was reminded what it was all about, namely, why do I in this life have the career that I do. I am a teacher. It is what I was meant to be, and martial arts is just my vehicle.

I began to read more books and look for other experiences. I signed up for an adult education class at the local high school. The instructor was teaching a psychic program which seemed to be energy based. My energy must just jump out at people no matter where I am because the instructor was going to do something with a deck of cards and picked me to go out in the hall. While I was gone he lined up some cards on a table and asked the students to gather around the table and as a group concentrate their energy onto one card. Then we would all see if I could feel which card they were thinking of.

I was called back into the room and asked to hold my hand over each of the cards and see if I felt anything. I slowly passed my hand over each card several times. There were two cards that I could feel energy rising from but finally I decided on the one with the greater amount of energy. The instructor was so disappointed but everyone else cheered. It seems they did not trust the instructor not to tell me which card so he was focused on the original one but everyone else had picked a different one and that was the one I chose.

Since I mention the word TRUST I need to say I am not as trusting as you think when you meet me. I still remain a skeptic about many things and as a teacher have been hurt more times than I can say by students who love me, think I am great, only to leave and do something else. Once a family left because I would not promote the older boy when he was unable to complete my criteria for a belt. They joined another school and the child was promoted to black belt and actually came to one of our tournaments to compete. I looked at him as he performed Sunsu Kata and groaned. He may have felt good about himself but he looked so bad that all I could think was I am glad he isn't wearing our patch.

I have found that the ones I can bring to a quality level karate student will also excel in other sports and all my hard work is lost when they decide to take the easier route. I am not an easy teacher but I am a caring one. I weigh what I see as a student's ability and try to bring them to their very best. If you are not a four year old there is no reason to baby you into learning. I offer a few corrections which I believe will make the student a better practitioner and if they do work it then they will most certainly improve to match the image they have of themselves in their mirrors at home.

Still, these students who go on to easier sports are more of the exception. For the most part the students I've lost have gone to college and moved on to their own careers, marriages and family. But, most have kept in touch one way or another, stopped in for a visit, sent cards and family photos and so on. One time a boy who left after his obtaining his yellow belt and later went into the military returned for a visit and told me he kept thinking of me the entire time in basic training and that got him through the rough times. Occasionally I also meet parents of former students who tell me about their children and the difference I have made in their lives. These moments are most precious to me. I especially love it when I start getting children of the children I have taught.

So do I trust many people? Not really, but I trust the result of our interaction will be in sync with what the Universe wanted for us. So, now I have learned to release and let go so that everyone can find their own path and grow. This isn't anything more than a parent would want for their children. Teach them well and allow them to live their own lives.

Knowledge is Power! It is so tempting as we begin to grow spiritually to want to share what you have learned with others. This is all well and good, but not everyone is ready to hear these things. We have a responsibility to remember to allow others to grow and discover on their own, but on that rare occasion when you find yourself conversing with someone who "gets it" that is wonderful, exciting and extremely uplifting.

Energy is strong and negative energy can physically hurt us. We can block negativity by putting up a mental barricade sort of like visualizing a giant letter X. But, as martial artists we have learned that blocks can not only be painful but they can keep you in that situation. As we mature in martial arts we learn, similar to a bull fighter, that it is better to shift and avoid an attack than meet it head on. In spirituality we can shift gears by making light of the situation or simply allow the negativity to flow through us and out the without accepting it into our lives. Bruce Lee said it best when he said, "Get rid of the people who suck the life out of you."

I took more meditation classes with a lady named Ann who opened up other avenues for me. She introduced me to the writings and predictions of Edgar Casey and his channeled down healing techniques and serums. I also met Francesca, a lady who sold crystals and stones at a local flea market. She is the one who eventually taught me the power of color and how to work with a crystal. Colors have palpable energy.

By visualizing certain colors you can effectively change a situation. As a small example if someone is giving you a difficult time you can visualize them wearing pink and green ribbons in their hair, love and heart energy. You not only relax your own energy with this funny picture but they too begin to change. I simultaneously began to learn about the energy of crystals and our power to divine and predict through their use, eventually incorporating it into my karate class as a way to demonstrate Ki.

Ann took me to meet Frank Alper in New York City whose meditations opened up more thoughts of Universal lessons. I discovered the workings of Kinesiology where our thought energy not only moves the crystal but can also weaken or strengthen a person around us.

One time I was driving someplace and the car in front of me was not making a turn on green when no one was coming. I tapped my horn and this so angered the man driving that he stopped his car in mid turn causing both of us to block a main road. He jumped out of his car and started screaming and cursing at me calling me an ugly mother f-er. People in cars nearby were shocked but I was angry and jumped out too, ready for whatever. But then I looked at this guy who had just called me an ugly mother f-er and it struck me so funny. He had this mass of curly uncombed hair, wearing sloppy clothing in an old car and I just started to laugh.

He got so mad that he got into his car and stormed away. Was that words or energy? I don't know but maybe it was a combination of both.

Sometimes we get a funny feeling about something and change our route only to hear later something happened on that road which could have been us if we hadn't turned away. Sometimes the Universe is protecting us by making us miss a plane that had engine trouble or crashed. These are not coincidences.

When I was first married and living in Flushing, Queens, I awoke one day with a feeling that I did not want to go to work that beautiful day. I convinced my husband to take a day off from work with me and surprisingly he agreed which believe me, was quite unusual. We went to the Bronx to go horseback riding and then to my parents for dinner. Suddenly the power went out. Not just in the Bronx either but throughout all of New York City. Not that we could know that from where we were. Thinking it was just the Bronx, we drove home on streets with no traffic lights. Thank heavens we were okay and also that our apartment was only one flight up as, of course, there was no elevator service. When I thought about it and the timing I would have been trapped for hours in the hot Subway by myself that day, if I hadn't paid attention to what the Universe was telling me. Sometimes listening to our inner feelings is the right thing to do especially if it is as strong as it was that day.

On another occasion when I was working in NYC as a medical technician in the Pathology department at Roosevelt Hospital I awoke with the feeling I needed to wear my diamond rings and a gold bracelet to work. I was in Histology so I rarely wore much jewelry as I was constantly using chemicals but that one day I did. When we got home our house had been robbed. All of my jewelry was gone, as well as an envelope of cash for our upcoming trip that had been labeled, ironically enough, "Take Me."

I used to meditate when I cleaned the house. For one thing I could pretend the maid came and did it instead of me as I soared away in my mind to somewhere else. One day I was vacuuming the living room floor and I had a strong desire to go down to the bluff near our house and walk on the beach. I told myself I had to finish cleaning and that I couldn't go until I was done. I cannot tell you how strong this desire to walk on the beach became other than to say I finally gave in, stopped what I was doing, and went for a walk on the beach. I brought our dog Poochie, a black and white husky lab mix, down there with me and we began to walk. We found a group of three girls that day on the beach with us. I could hear them telling their friend that it was okay to do things alone. Then I heard, "Let's ask this lady."

They came up to me and said their friend was afraid to do anything by herself and was that the same for me? I told them if I want to do something I will just do it even if I prefer to go with a friend. It seems that was what she needed to hear and they were happy with the conversation. I started to walk a little further when I realized the desire was no longer there. I was meant to go down to the beach and help this girl who I had never met. Once I did as I was driven to do, it was fine for me to return home and finish my cleaning. This was definitely not like me at all. Why do things like that happen? The answer is sometimes we are needed elsewhere and the Universe finds a way to get us there. We can't argue with the Universe so when something feels right do it and conversely if something does not feel right get away from the situation as fast as you can.

It is possible to open up to spiritual occurrences to the point where you begin to doubt yourself or the existence of something we cannot see. At those times you will find yourself pulling away for a while. That is okay, and natural, because so much seems to happen that it can become scary. Little things like thinking about someone you have not seen in a long time who suddenly calls or sends you a letter. Other times when you call them, they were just thinking of you. Once I was teaching a karate class and the idea of unusual occurrences came up when one of the former students who had not been gone that long walked in and they said look Sensei Brian is here. I said well it's not like he has been gone all that long, but if Melissa were to walk in that would definitely be something. A few minutes later when we went on to other things and I was distracted I heard, "Sensei, Melissa is here." Can you imagine my surprise when Melissa who had been away for years showed up!

While I am on the subject of Spiritual happenings when we least expect them, I need to add another story. If you read the beginning of the book you will understand why I was very attached to my Mom and took her passing rather hard. Here I am talking about all kinds of spiritual stuff and I could never get the feeling of her presence or any real message from her. One day Hanshi Adler and I were traveling to a tournament in Orlando. We arrived at the airport and checked our bags for the flight. I overheard there was a flight to Palm Beach leaving before ours and I thought, I wish I was on that one because that is where my parents are buried. When we arrived in Orlando Sensei's bags came off the carousel but mine did not. I went to the office and was told, "Don't worry we know where your bags are, they went to Palm Beach." I thought, wow that was just what I was thinking about.

I went to the ladies room and thought about this coincidence when suddenly I remembered the date was August 16th. I had forgotten it was Mom's birthday. Then as clear as a bell I heard my mom's voice in my head saying, "You wanted a message. Is this loud enough?"

When I spoke about karate earlier in this book I mentioned leaving the dojo early one night because Muhammad Ali was fighting. This was also the first time I needed to show my confidence and determination when confronted by someone who I found threatening. Another time when I was being inducted into the Jewish Sports Hall of Fame I entered the Lobby to find a Giant cut-out of yup - Ali. It seems in one way or another he was there on many turns in my life. None more profoundly than the time I went on an elementary school trip to New York City with my son Steven's class.

We went to the Empire State Building and Ripley's Believe It or Not. My husband, Ralph, was working not far away in the city at that time and came to meet us. He led us back to Penn Station on a different route than we had originally taken. As we were walking I felt something change – it was an energy that stopped me dead in my tracks. I looked to my right and as I write this, try to visualize what was happening. I looked up a flight of stairs and first saw a pair of shiny shoes, the bottom of Tuxedo pants and a walking stick. As my eyes traveled further up I realized I was looking at Muhammad Ali.

Yes. That Muhammad Ali.

Understand that I never recognize anyone from photos or TV but this was Ali – The Greatest. My mouth dropped probably down to my toes. Ali looked down at this gawking person, put out his hand and said, "It's you." We shook hands and then he threw some punches at the kids before being whisked away in a waiting Limo. The charisma and energy of this man is something I remember to this day. Even during his fight with Parkinson's his sprit was strong and his kind and caring ways shone through. This then is the energy I refer to as Spiritual. the power to overcome obstacles and the aura that is palpable around one.

And by the way, the day I received the rose from my dear friend Don Bohan I returned home to find my autographed cover of Gentleman Quartly fom Ali in the mail.

Dr Terrence Webster-Doyle is another person on a similar path to mine and an example of what I consider synchronistic happenings.

In the 80s I came upon a book called "Karate: The Art of Empty Self." I enjoyed reading it very much and thought to myself that it reflected exactly what I thought and felt. But, being busy trying to stay focused on technique, teaching and getting the dojo on track I put it aside and basically forgot about it.

Many years later one of my students came to me and said, "Sensei, I just read a book and it reminded me of you, so much of what you teach is in it." I asked him about the book and he showed it to me. As I browsed through the book I realized it was the same one I had read many years before. I realized that focusing so much on trying to be a good martial artist I was starting to get off my true path toward enlightenment. It hit me so strong that I felt compelled to try and contact the author. By trial and error I managed to find a phone number for him and called. I told the person who answered that I needed to contact the author because he had just re-affirmed what I had believed all along. She said, "Okay he is here now." Wow, I thought. What were the odds of that? I was almost late getting to the dojo that night as I did not want to stop our conversation. When you find someone who thinks and believes as you do I recommend treasuring every minute of it.

Coincidence? We seem to be meant to "accidentally" meet people on similar paths or pulled in one direction or another. All of these "coincidences" are yet another reminder for us to stay on path each time we get lost. But, we also have to be both open to the possibilities and willing to take a chance.

After a while I found myself busy with life and off my spiritual path. Nothing seemed to go smoothly and I was not able to focus or meditate. A coffee shop had opened up next door to the dojo so I stopped in one day. On the counter was a flyer for a "Spiritual Journey Within" weekend with Doctor

Bill Bezman. It looked interesting but who was this person? My skepticism immediately kicked in. I knew I had to get back to finding myself, but who was this person and what was this seminar? I called the number and spoke to the secretary and told her I do not like other people messing with my mind especially if I never met them. She put him on the phone and I was invited to the office to chat. I told him I was interested but if I did not like how it was going I would leave. He said he understood but did not feel I would be disappointed.

The weekend came and what I really remember from it was an opening lecture and a meditation. I was so tense that I did not get anything he said but I saw some clouds and had some feelings and described a scene when suddenly the woman across from me said that is what she saw, too.

Bill told me I locked into her meditation and that was why I saw it. The weekend brought me back to my reality of working with a variety of mostly healing arts. Through Doctor Bezman at Pathways to Health I learned to intensify these healing abilities until I became part of a group that would offer free healings once a month. We would do a group meditation setting the intent to be used as an instrument of healing. If we achieved a healing it was not us, but the Universe working through us. In many cases it was as if miracles were happening. Sometimes we are not meant to heal just to relieve pain or pressure. Many illnesses are Karmic and something people are meant to go through them without us ever knowing why.

Once a patient came in complaining of abdominal pain and wanted help with it. I passed my hands above her body and could not feel the pain where she said she had it but I did feel a very heavy dark area around her heart. I kept trying to send a healing where she said but each time I approached her heart I felt pain and darkness until I wanted to cry. As we began to chat I asked her casually what was happening and she told me her mother was very sick, and began to cry. As she did I asked her to let go of that emotion and was able to use my energy to release the pressure on her chest and heart. I figured I failed in curing what hurt her but when she was ready to leave she said she no longer had any pain anywhere.

When working with energy like this it is important to first protect yourself and second to recognize if you experience that person's pain to recognize it as not your own, and let go of it. On another occasion Doctor Bezman held one of our healing group meetings at a restaurant. As we began to work one healing aspect on each other the owner came and asked for help because one of the waiters spilled boiling hot water on his hand which was beet red even after having been under cold water and ice. Doctor Bezman told me to work on his hand while everyone else continued with the class. Why me? There was no way I could help this man but if he wanted my help the least I could do was try. I passed my energy over the red area of his hand and it felt like it could burn me but I thought I shall not absorb his pain but allow it to go through me and release it and that was how I started. When you pass your hands above someone for a healing you also need to wipe the energy off so you do not receive their pain. I did that a few times and then began to visualize his hand cooling down and healing. I am not sure how long I worked on him but when I opened my eyes once more and asked how he was, he said he felt so much better and his hand no longer hurt or looked as beet red. I also found out the following day his hand did not blister.

Soon after I met Doctor Bezman he had begun to go to the Patricia Hayes Institute, Delphi University, North Georgia to train with a healing technique called RoHun. Bill is a Psychotherapist and also trained in Hypnotherapy. He said where Psychotherapy could take three years to create a healing and Hypnotherapy three months, with RoHun a healing occurs almost immediately. They had created a channeled down set of healing cards – I believe they were from Arthur Ford – and Bill had become an instructor so he offered a course to his healers and I became certified in RoHun.

This is a type of healing that uses a process to locate a fault in a person's chakra and the issue in the person's lifetime from which the fault came. A chakra is similar to a wheel hidden within critical junctures within the body. There's seven chakras, each symbolizing different emotions. By doing this along with specific meditations a person becomes capable of viewing a particular troubling feeling and releasing it, thus creating a healing. I suggest if this is of interest to you to read books like "Wheels of Life" by Anodea Judith.

Remember that people who are healers, like I am, are simply acting as vehicles for a higher force to work. When working with clients this way the results never cease to amaze me. People I would think never had a jealous thought in their head find they indeed had a moral dilemma or an impure thought and it was weighing them down. I worked once with a man who asked for a healing. I do not know what is bothering most clients or what they need I just let the process unfold. When I asked him who the person was that he could see from his past life, he said it was a Nun. I was shocked but went with it. It seemed the Nun had to let some people leave the convent and was having a rough time with it. In the end I found out that the business he owned was struggling and he needed to let some people go. He was having a rough time of it just like the Nun was. Once the thought of the Nun was released from his past he felt relief and was able to move on from it.

While I was working with RoHun I had my spirit guide helping me. You remember, the one who was mad at me in Sedona. We were doing great and I was growing and learning in leaps and bounds, but as I was doing a healing one day he started to tell me he had to go. I finished the healing and called Bill right away. I was so upset. My guide wanted to leave and I could never do this alone. Bill suggested I meditate and ask my guide to show me who would replace him.

It seems there are times when we have learned all that a guide can teach us and it is time to move to someone higher. In karate there are some who leave their sensei thinking they know it all. In most cases it is just ego that makes them leave and they never grow after that. Sometimes, a smart student will move on from one sensei to another to learn more. But, it was different with my guide because it was him who said I had outgrown him and it was time to move on.

From RoHun I also began to train in Past Life Regression. I had already been regressed to a time where I was the King's son and had to go to battle so I knew what it was like. With practice I had gone back to some other times as well. Part of the course was that we had to do several past life readings and report on them. That weekend was our Karate Camp and my friend Linda had come up from Virginia to train and stay a few days after with me. My son, Steven, was home that summer so the three of us went out on the boat.

Linda said I could do a past life on her so we started the process but then Steven began talking so Linda stopped. The amazing thing was that all three of our lives were connected in that same life time. Steven was the King and Linda was a servant in our household. I think we were all shocked at this outcome.

As I was doing all of these things I also began reading books like the Tao Te Ching, an ancient Chinese text and drawing wisdom from the English translation I found myself using different divining tools or oracles. The major one was the I Ching. I purchased "The Illustrated I Ching by L. Wing." As a matter of note for any Isshinryu Practitioners reading this part, Master Shimabuku Tatsuo was not just a great karate master but also a fortune teller. It is my understanding that he used sticks to divine answers. The I Ching uses tossed coins to create a hexagram and then teaches one to translate the meaning for the question asked. When I needed to form a corporation for my dojo I also wanted to combine it with RoHun and other healing modalities. I could not think of a word to use so eventually I decided on the coin method through the I Ching. The result was "Synergy." Combining two things and making one that is stronger than either could be by themselves. Perfect! It is what I had always wanted, to combine spirituality with martial arts.

Earlier I brought up the subject of cards that were channeled down to make healing easier through RoHun. Spiritual Channeling is amazing to see and Judith Grant became a Channel for an entity called Balistar. Bali was a delightful entity who is from the Pleiades. He answered to elders so if you asked a question to which one should not know the answer the council would tell Bali not to say. I love Balistar and his delightful ways of answering questions or giving information. One day he told me that he was a part of me as well. We are many and yet we are one. We are all connected to one another as we are connected to the Universal force. So I thought that was what he meant but he said no, a part of me is in you. I have always been with you. I helped you as a child when your bicycle turned upside down and brought you down safely. He told me when I was born my soul purpose was to heal and to help my dying father. But, I was a child and in those days children were to be seen and not heard so I was kept away from my father which left me frustrated. Now I have finally found my soul purpose in healing. Bali has become my guide in many ways and yes, he is there for me when I do any healings.

One day my friend Kathy, was visiting and I took her with me to a Bali Channeling. She told me on the way that she had to go to the post office. I said sure, but *after* we go. We were talking and I drove past my turn and had to make a U turn to go back. I found a large opening and went in to turn and she said "Marilyn, this is a post office." We mailed the letter and went to see Bali who spoke to the group and later to us individually. When It was my turn Bali said, "I know you. I always know you. I like to ride in the car with you and you forgot so I made you go to the post office." That definitely blew me and my friend away. At a later time I was told the council said he could not ride with me anymore. Sad to hear but I sometimes think of him and feel he is beside me in the car or airplane. Bali sure loved to fly. Unfortunately Judith no longer channels on a regular basis.

There is power in meditating with like-minded people and for the longest time I would have monthly meditations in my dojo for whoever was interested. At times they were very powerful. After each meditation I would ask everyone to tell me what they saw. One lady who was seated across from me went on to describe what she saw and then said the most unusual thing happened. "At the end of my meditation a tiny black dog came bouncing in and around us." I knew without a doubt it was our first 5 pound black phantom toy poodle Pierre.

Dogs are truly God's gift or else why would dog spelt backwards spell God. I do not believe there is another creature that can give such unconditional love and forgiveness than a dog. Don't get me wrong I love horses, birds, and turtles as well as many other kinds of animals. Each are indeed loving, but, I do not think they reach the same level as that of a dog.

I have been told that it is unusual for a dog that we loved to come back and visit but one night I was meditating on the word love and as I was about to fall asleep I heard the sound of our second Dog, Poochie, a husky lab mix coming into the bedroom. I saw him at the base of our bed and was about to say what are you doing in here when daddy is home when I suddenly realized our Pomeranian, Max, was sleeping by my head. It struck me that Poochie, our rescue dog, had come to remind me of unconditional love as he was the epitome of just that. He was not a perfect dog but he was our most loving dog.

Years later when Max was 16 1/2 his life with us was over. Yet another heartbreak. You have to wonder what God was thinking giving us such loving creatures with such a short lifespan. All I can think is it is a reminder that nothing is permanent and to learn to deal with such heart wrenching hurt. We were going to try and live without a dog for a while as it is difficult to travel to as many places as we would like. I had already planned a trip to see the kids and another to Disney with the entire family so I figured after March I would look for a small poodle mix dog to rescue.

That December I went to see a psychic. I asked her about Max and she said she does not read dogs. She went on to talk to me about other things and then toward the end she said, "you are going to get another dog soon." I said, "No probably not for a year but I want to try for sooner." She replied, "No, sooner than that and that puppy has already been born and your previous dog knows and approves of it."

Casey was born on November 30th and we got him January 26th, two days before our trip to see the kids. In the beginning of that same January I had a beautiful dream about Max. I was so happy to see him and be with him again I did not want to wake up. But, then in the dream it was his last day again and I started crying in my sleep. I woke up sobbing. as I got myself together I realized It was a dream but then I heard the sound of water running. My husband was asleep so I started checking the bathrooms and kitchen finally going down to the basement and discovered the entire place under several inches of water. The washing machine hose had broken. Was it coincidence or did Max come to wake me up before it got any worse?

I am not an expert on any of the ideas presented here nor do I ever claim to be. I am on a journey of discovery just like you. This type of exploration combined with my interest in the martial arts has brought me to the level of growth I have achieved at this moment in time. This chapter is an attempt to explain how I was able to connect the energy of the universe and the route I took to discover my place in this giant puzzle we call life.

People in Asia grow up in much of what I began to experience, but we as Americans do not. It was through this exploration that I was able to form a link from the spiritual into the practical we call karate. And, like my corporation name, Synergy, combining these two things has made me better than I could possibly have been with only one piece of my puzzle. When we meditate the students are taught to look around the area they find themselves in and often receive a better understanding of our past or current situation.

I do not suggest what I did or experienced is right for you but I do suggest if any of this has piqued your interest please do follow up with it. There is so much more to be learned and experienced in life. Each of us is connected by that one spark of Universal light and by opening up to this connection we can experience Limitless Possibilities.

While much of my spiritual journey was personal, I

did share some of my learnings and methods with students. I also wrote about the connections between karate and the spiritual on rare occasions.

Eventually I wrote a piece called "The Limitless Spirit of the Martial Arts." I submitted it to Taekwondo Times which was a top publication at the time. I remember I had taken a bunch of photos of seagulls and tried to superimpose them on a yin yang symbol to accompany the piece. I hate to admit it, but it was not looking good. But, I was determined. I wrote a letter to Taekwondo Times telling them that I wanted people to know about determination and belief and how it is present in the martial arts. I sent a photo of me with my tonfa so they would know who I was and the one page story with my disastrous photos of the seagulls.

To my surprise, within the month, a copy of Taekwondo Times arrived at my house with my piece right there on the front. They had fixed my photo and included it at the top of my little story on the right hand side of the magazine and printed my photo full size on the left. As I write this I have to catch my breath remembering how awesome that felt. This is a form of energy in itself. Joy, pride, determination... These all come from our ki and it is up to us to decide what we will do with our energy.

In 1992 I brought a team of "athletes" to the Junior Maccabi Games in Baltimore, Maryland. I use the term athletes loosely because there wasn't even a tryout. Whoever wanted to participate, could. It was a crazy time and the event turned into an international one. The Mexican team had obviously put in the training time and our Suffolk County JCC competitors were no match for them.

While we were at the event I was working with the students in the courtyard outside the cafeteria. There I received the best compliment I had ever gotten. Tables were set up in the room across from the cafeteria so I went in to look. A few seconds after entering I heard someone call "Sensei." I looked around to see a Hasidic Jewish man standing there. I said "How did you know I was a Sensei?" His answer stays with me to this day: "The way you walked told me you are a Sensei."

Our ki shines through our physical selves. If your ki is weak, it shows. If your ki is strong, that will show, too. Remember what I said about self-defense? Don't look like you're a victim. Act with assurance. Stride when you walk. Keep your head up and meet the eyes of everyone around you. Let your ki shine through, and in this way you will let it grow strong.

Marilyn Fierro

Index

63295518R00164